Ed Stafford's
ULTIMATE ADVENTURE GUIDE

A Firefly Book

Published by Firefly Books Ltd. 2018

First printing

Publisher Cataloging-in-Publication Data (U.S.)

Library of Congress Control Number: 2018942046

Library and Archives Canada Cataloguing in Publication

Stafford, Ed, author
     Ed Stafford's ultimate adventure guide : the bucket list
for the brave / Ed Stafford.
ISBN 978-0-228-10160-4 (softcover)
     1. Adventure travel--Guidebooks. 2. Extreme sports-- Guidebooks. 3. Outdoor recreation--Guidebooks. 4. Travel-- Guidebooks. 5. Guidebooks. I. Title. II. Title: Ultimate adventure guide.
G516.S73 2018   910.2'02   C2018-902375-9

Published in the United States by
Firefly Books (U.S.) Inc.
P.O. Box 1338, Ellicott Station
Buffalo, New York 14205

Published in Canada by
Firefly Books Ltd.
50 Staples Avenue, Unit 1
Richmond Hill, Ontario L4B 0A7

Printed in China

Originally published by Collins
An imprint of HarperCollins Publishers
Westerhill Road
Bishopbriggs
Glasgow G64 2QT

Ed Stafford's

ULTIMATE ADVENTURE GUIDE

The Bucket List for the Brave

Ed Stafford

FIREFLY BOOKS

FOREWORD

I first heard of Ed Stafford when he was on an expedition in South America that would eventually see him walk the Amazon River from source to sea. I was serving as a trustee of the Transglobe Expedition Trust, a charity that provides support to ground-breaking feats of exploration, and was considering whether to provide a grant for this seemingly outrageous venture. It was the firm belief of the experts I spoke with at the time that completing such an endeavour, fraught with danger and natural obstacles as it was, would be impossible.

Ed, walking first with Luke Collyer and then Gadiel 'Cho' Sanchez, was to prove the experts wrong and completed his Amazon walk in 860 days. It is an achievement that deserves to be regarded among the highest feats of exploration and Ed has continued to follow his own arduous and uncomfortable path ever since.

He has undertaken distinctive trials of endurance and survival skills in many of the world's most hostile places, from desert to jungle to frozen lands, and proved himself to be one of the most accomplished adventurers of his generation. I am proud to say that he has since joined me as a trustee of the Transglobe Expedition Trust.

The challenges set out in this book vary greatly but they are linked by a common thread. They all encourage the reader to discover the emotional and spiritual rewards a person can best experience when exposed to genuine risk.

It is, in my view, impossible to derive the fullest satisfaction from any adventure if it is devoid of the element of danger. In a modern culture where we are constantly encouraged to be risk-averse in our day-to-day lives, the opportunity to test our reactions to extremes has become somewhat limited, to the detriment of our individual selves and society as a whole. It is my hope that, in reading these entries, a spark of curiosity will ignite a lust for adventure in the reader.

Should this book inspire you to devise an expedition of your own, and your dream requires funds to get it off the ground, then Ed, our fellow Transglobe Expedition Trustees and I would meet to see if your plans qualify for a grant. But be warned, to gain the favour of the trustees your proposed expedition has to be 'mad but marvellous'.

I am particularly pleased to read that Ed has found room in this book for two ventures, both of which I have undertaken, that encapsulate the rewards of risk. The Marathon des Sables, an ultra-distance race through the High Atlas Mountains of Morocco, is a brutal examination of endurance. The North Face of the Eiger, a rock face which has brought tragic ends to so many who have attempted it, is a prolonged test of nerve and skill. Participating in both of these exploits has given me deep satisfaction, as I'm sure it will to others, too.

I am equally glad that, among the scheduled events and recognised challenges, Ed has also found room for adventures that are much less structured in scope, such as charting a course through rainforest, as sometimes it is these unregulated forays into the unknown that can be the most rewarding of all.

So I commend this book with the hope that it motivates everyone who reads it to consider how he or she can live a life that incorporates a spirit of adventure and I wish you a good read and many happy travels.

Ranulph Fiennes

CONTENTS

CONTENTS

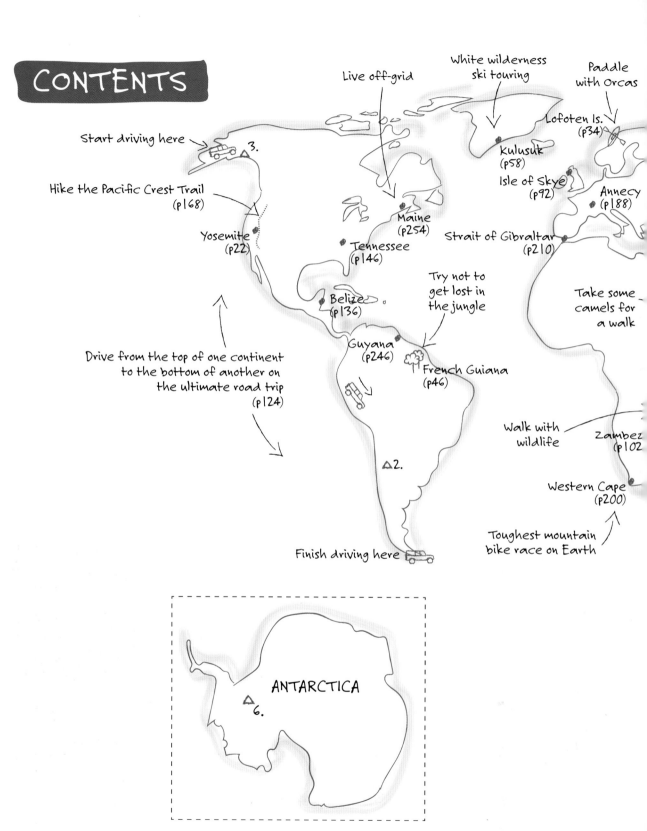

Start driving here

Hike the Pacific Crest Trail
(p168)

Yosemite
(p22)

Drive from the top of one continent
to the bottom of another on
the ultimate road trip
(p124)

3.

Live off-grid

White wilderness
ski touring

Paddle
with Orcas

Lofoten Is.
(p34)

Kulusuk
(p58)

Isle of Skye
(p92)

Annecy
(p188)

Maine
(p254)

Tennessee
(p146)

Strait of Gibraltar
(p210)

Try not to
get lost in
the jungle

Take some
camels for
a walk

Belize
(p136)

Guyana
(p246)

French Guiana
(p46)

Walk with
wildlife

Zambez
(p102)

Western Cape
(p200)

Toughest mountain
bike race on Earth

△2.

Finish driving here

ANTARCTICA

△
6.

Swim in
freezing
water

Lake Baikal
(p68)

Climb the second
seven summits
(p230)

1. K2
2. Ojos del Salado
3. Mount Logan
4. Mount Kenya
5. Dykh-Tau
6. Mount Tyree
7. Puncak Mandala

5.

1.

Yunnan Province
(p178)

Live with
Shaolin monks

India
(p80)

The Danakil
(p158)

4.

Cycle across
India

North Luangwa
(p218)

7.

Raft the North Johnstone River

Vava'u Tonga
(p114)

Survive on a
desert island

Good rock
climbing here

STAR QUALITY

Throughout the book, you'll notice that each of the adventures has been given a star grading from 1-5 in three categories; DIFFICULTY, ENDURANCE and NERVES OF STEEL.

The ratings are supposed to give you some concept of the physical and mental toll each expedition will take on you but, for goodness' sake, don't take them too literally. Everybody has different capabilities, and this is very much my perspective on things.

This breakdown will put it in context for you:

★☆☆☆☆ Bloody tough

★★☆☆☆ Really bloody tough

★★★☆☆ Exceptionally bloody tough

★★★★☆ Turn-your-hair-white tough

★★★★★ People will write books about you

INTRODUCTION

The spirit of adventure is an amazing thing. At its simplest level, it's a quality that will bring lots of fun into your life, help you to see incredible sights and become friends with some interesting people. It will spur you on to explore the world around you which, in turn, will provide a brainful of memories to dive into and cherish for the rest of your life.

However, there's much more to it than that. It's something more important and more profound, too. Tapping into your sense of adventure, feeding it and letting it grow, can make you a better, more humble, version of yourself.

Travelling to some of the world's most extreme places; testing my body, mind and soul in challenging conditions; and learning how to get through them, has shaped my entire life.

It's helped me evolve as a person in all sorts of different ways. At times, it's been simply appreciating the value of humility and being respectful to the people and cultures I encounter. I've had to learn practical skills, too, and it's incredible how much inner confidence you can muster just by knowing you have the ability to solve a problem.

On other occasions, it's been a lot more complicated. I've been in places where my mind and spirit have been put under pressure and I've been forced to find a way of resolving inner turmoil. That's not always easy to do but sometimes it takes an extreme situation to confront some of the issues that hold you back in your life. It can be tough but it can also be cathartic. Reaching a better understanding of your inner self can be difficult to do when wrapped up in day-to-day life. Sometimes you have to get out of your comfort zone to move forward.

I started writing this book with a very clear purpose in mind. I wanted to encourage people to make room for exploits that give them a sense of fulfilment only really attainable when there's an element of risk. At times it becomes easy to settle into a comfort zone. We get into routines that become harder to break the longer we follow them. Then, before we know it, time has marched on and we have missed an opportunity to do something that will truly lift our spirits.

One of my favourite things is planning an expedition. Pulling together all the various arrangements that need to be made; feeling the anticipation mount as another bit of your plan clicks in to place; that little skip in your heart as you tick off another day until your journey begins – I love it all.

The entries in this book are designed to get your senses twitching in the same way. None of them are easy. They all involve an element of danger and each will test your character. If you're going to attempt any of them, you'll need to put the hours in first.

What you won't find in these pages are specific instructions on 'how to have an adventure'. You'll need to decide how to approach your travels for yourself. We're all different after all.

What I hope you *will* find is a colourful portrait of what it feels like to be out there, taking risks and pushing yourself to the limit in incredible places. I've tried to convey some of the emotions that make being out there so addictive – the elation when you finally get a fire going without matches or fuel; the mix of relief and exhilaration when a rain shower comes and replenishes your dwindling water supplies; the delayed rush of satisfaction that comes when you look back at a dizzyingly high mountain ridge and recall how you traversed it earlier that day. Hopefully one or two passages will raise a smile, too. You don't have to take yourself too seriously just because you're embarking on a serious venture!

Some of the entries are challenges I've undertaken myself. Surviving for two months on

a desert island was one of the hardest and most rewarding things I've ever experienced. I've tried to offer some idea of the psychological pressure that living in total isolation can trigger but also a taste of the joys that are part and parcel of such an intense exploit. Picking two points on a map and walking between them, as we showcase on page 46, is the kind of idiosyncratic challenge that gives me a buzz. The thought that you could well be the only person, in the history of

humanity, to have picked a certain route through an untouched wilderness is pretty cool.

Other adventures are drawn from my own personal bucket list, such as contemplating an attempt on the majestic but deadly summit of K2 or plotting a grand cycling tour across the Indian subcontinent.

This book offers a mix of endeavours. Some can conceivably be tackled at fairly short notice, if you're willing to commit to proper training and preparation. Others are once-in-a-lifetime challenges that will consume you for years.

I've tried to strike the same balance between great expeditions and spontaneous escapades in my own life, too. Walking the Amazon took nearly three years and, unsurprisingly, had a pretty profound effect on my life. Since then things have changed. I'm married now and have a son, but we're determined to continue to make room for adventures. Partly this is because there are still so many incredible challenges to be tackled and fascinating corners of the world to explore that it would be impossible to stop exploring. But it's also because I know it will be good for me, and for my family. By going into the unknown and facing whatever challenges are thrown at us, we'll be happier, stronger and more rounded people.

I hope you'll find the same sense of fulfilment from your own travels. And if this book should play some small part in inspiring one of your future adventures, I'd be thrilled to know more about it. You can contact me via www.edstafford.org.

Good luck and never let the naysayers put you off.

Ed Stafford

Leicestershire, England, 2018

A QUICK WORD OF CAUTION

If you decide to undertake an expedition you must acknowledge to yourself that you, and you alone, are responsible for anything going wrong. This book is meant to inspire and encourage you to live the fullest and most rewarding life possible. It will only be that way if you stop looking to blame others and accept that your life is the way it is because of your own thoughts and actions.

Each of the entries carries a certain element of danger and some carry a risk to life. Therefore, it is essential that you carefully consider the threats to your wellbeing, and that of others, before you embark on your travels. That means spending time studying the nature of the dangers you'll face. It means being honest about your own abilities and the ability of other people in your party, if applicable. It means having carefully-planned contingencies in place in case something goes wrong and you need help.

If there wasn't a risk, it wouldn't be an adventure - it would be a game. You must let that sink in and decide if you are prepared to accept that risk. If you are - and if you take responsibility to manage those risks skilfully - your life just got a whole lot richer.

INSPIRING STORIES

Many of these entries are drawn from my own personal experience. For instance, I really did have to chase after a camel in the hottest place on Earth! In other cases, I've used the incredible feats of fellow adventurers as a source of inspiration. One of these heroes is an explorer called Laura Bingham. In 2018, along with two her fellow travellers Pip Stewart and Ness Knight, she became the first person ever to navigate the longest river in Guyana, the Essequibo, from source to sea. It's a great example of exploration in the modern age and Laura – who also happens to be my wife – was good enough to share an insight into this incredible journey.

Elsewhere I've drawn from the great feats of history, such as the incredible attempts to scale the murderous North Face of the Eiger, and cited examples of people who continue to break new ground and set new standards, such as the inspirational cold-water swimmer, Lewis Pugh. I find these stories of real-life heroism hugely inspiring and I hope you will, too.

TRAVEL MANIFESTO

Each of the adventures featured here requires a degree of planning and a lot of specific training. Preparing for an expedition is a skill in itself; experience will improve your effectiveness, as will finding the right people and listening to their advice.

In this section, I've tried to think of all the useful advice I can offer. Some parts are general observations and others are fairly specific but all of the information below is based on techniques and ways of working that have helped me. Hopefully they'll help you, too.

STRENGTH & CONDITIONING

There are one or two trips in here where physical fitness is not a particular requirement. On the Pacific Crest Trail, for instance, you can hike yourself fit as you go. For the majority of them, however, a reasonable standard of conditioning is going to be necessary.

The best way to prepare is to practise what you're going to be doing i.e. if you're heading on a long-distance cycling expedition, spend as much time as you can in the saddle with your bike rigged out in travel mode. You'll get a feel for the conditions and be developing the muscles you'll be using the most. Crucially, it will also give you a feel for the parts of your body that will come under the most strain and allow you to work out how to deal with that. Going to the gym might get you beach body ready but it's not necessarily the most effective use of your time.

One of the key areas of conditioning that I believe is often wrongly overlooked is suppleness. The ability to control the way your body moves is really important. If you're going to be stepping down off logs or boulders, crouching under tree limbs or squeezing through narrow gaps, all with a heavy rucksack on your back, it's important you can manage your body weight efficiently.

GET SMART

It's a GPS, a compass, a camera, a map, a video recorder, an MP3 player, a notebook, a torch ... and you can (sometimes) make phone calls on it, too. The smartphone has revolutionized adventure travel. If I was walking the Amazon again today I probably wouldn't bother with conventional cameras. A decent phone and a *GoPro* will do the job perfectly well and save you a huge amount of space and weight in your pack.

Your camera can be hugely useful, not just to record your adventure but also as an aide-mémoire. It only takes a second to snap a quick image of a sign, or a timetable, or a prominent landmark that you can use for navigation.

The latest generation of portable chargers and lightweight solar panels means your entire journey can be coordinated and catalogued through a few USB points. Ironically, one of the few things you can't always rely on your smartphone for is making calls. In the most remote places, it pays to have a satellite phone with you, too.

UN-LOSING YOURSELF

Getting lost is almost a kind of occupational hazard if you immerse yourself in the wild. The important thing is to devise a plan of action that allows you to regain control of the situation.

Set up a base; create a space where you know you can start a fire and camp for the night, if necessary. Make the base distinctive, clear a reasonable amount of space for your camp, then start exploring your surroundings in a measured way.

I would advocate a system called the Star Method. Take a compass bearing and walk 50 yards north, carefully noting any distinctive landmarks you come across, then track back to camp. Do the same for south, east and west, landscape permitting. Keep following the same procedure, going further every time before returning to base, until you can use your notes to form a picture of the surrounding landscape that corresponds with the features on a map.

FIRED UP

A fire is a bit like a dog. It can be a comfort, a protector and a useful companion but if you mistreat it... beware because it can lash out and hurt you.

Getting a fire going when you're alone in the wild is a real morale-booster. It's a source of heat and light, of course, and on a very basic level it gives you a reassuring feeling that you are making a go of things.

If you're serious about spending a lot of time in the wilderness, it's worth investing in some proper bushcraft training with someone who

knows what they're doing. Over four or five days you'll learn a lot about how to start a blaze without a lighter, how to get dry wood in wet conditions and so on.

When it comes to essential travel kit, I'd say a lighter is a close second behind a knife in terms of importance. I wouldn't go on an expedition without one.

DON'T OVERDRESS

I'm the last person to dish out fashion advice but, in my experience, it does pay to be self-aware about the way you dress and what it says about you. If you pitch up somewhere

MOTOR SKILLS

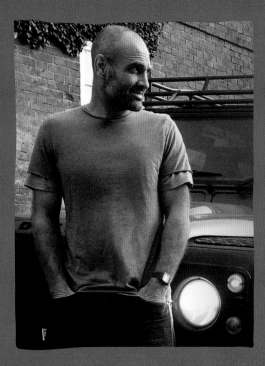

To make sure you keep moving in even the toughest circumstances, here are some general driving and vehicle-care tips that I've picked up from the experts at Land Rover:

* Make sure you're familiar with the equipment on the vehicle – not knowing how your winch works when you are already in trouble is always going to spoil your day.

* Take the right car for the job. Assess the terrain you'll be traversing and make sure your vehicle is the appropriate size. Does it have decent ground clearance? Will I need the extra traction offered by four-wheel drive? Is the fuel range good enough?

* Make sure you'll be able to get your hands on the right type (and quality) of fuel.

* Prepare for the very worst conditions you're likely to experience, even if they'll account for a small portion of the overall trip.

* Make sure you've dealt with any known issues or weaknesses before setting out. Old batteries die quickly in cold conditions; rocks will rip through tyres if the sidewalls are UV degraded.

* Tyres are always a compromise of various characteristics on multi-terrain expeditions. Asses your likely route to find the right balance.

* Keep your vehicle's centre of gravity low and the emergency kit accessible. An expedition roof rack covered in wheels, jerry cans and duffel bags may look cool, but it's terrible for stability.

* Make sure you are as capable as your vehicle. Do you have the appropriate driving skills and qualifications? If not, go on an off-road driving course.

looking like a model for an outdoor clothing catalogue – all expedition shirts, zip-off trousers and vented travel hats – you're creating a bit of a barrier because I can pretty much guarantee the local people you meet won't be wearing that stuff.

It might seem a small thing but it does say something about you and your approach to travel. Nowadays I invariably pack a few T-shirts, a couple of pairs of shorts and trousers and pick up anything else I need from a local store or market. It helps me feel more comfortable and less out of place.

MEDICAL MATTERS

I'm not a doctor and wouldn't presume to give anyone medical advice. Before you undertake any large-scale travelling you should get a full medical assessment from an expert. I'd certainly want advice on which antiseptics and antibiotics to carry with me; travelling without them is a risk you don't need to take.

When it comes to medical equipment, slimming things down to the bare essentials is a good idea. You can end up packing massive amounts of medical supplies, to try and cover every eventuality, and end up lugging about lots of kit you never use. Think about products that can fulfil a number of uses. Duct tape, for example, always comes in handy. Combine it with toilet paper and it makes a decent field dressing; you can use it with a slice of foam mattress to make a neck brace and wrap it round a stick to make a splint.

Superglue was originally devised as a field treatment for cuts and gashes and it's still a useful means of repairing yourself, as well as your equipment. Rather than overloading with medical supplies from the outset, I'd look to top-up my stocks en route. It saves on weight

and also forces you to consider, from the outset, whether each piece of equipment is *really* essential.

LEARN SOME CULTURE

During my walk through the Amazon, I reached an area of Peru known as the Red Zone. It had been a war zone, basically, for many years and the indigenous people had been subjected to atrocities by a group of communist guerrillas known as the Shining Path.

I knew nothing about this violent background when I arrived – most of the preparation I had done had been focused on arranging maps and kit. When I stumbled across this area and these people, who were effectively suffering from a communal form of post-traumatic stress disorder, I wasn't in a position to recognise what they'd experienced and how it would have an impact on the way they engaged with people visiting the area. That lack of cultural awareness is something I really regret; had I known more about what these people had been through I would have approached things very differently.

Now I always make a point of doing some research into the culture and history of an area before I travel there. A factor in this is language. I always try to learn a few key phrases of the local dialect before visiting a new region. Being able to thank someone, or ask for their help, in their local tongue is a sign of respect and humility that I find is universally appreciated.

YOU'VE GOT TO HAVE FAITH

Sometimes when people share their expedition plans with me I'm a bit perturbed by how much of their journey is pre-planned. While undertaking some research into the area you're visiting is desirable (see above), nailing

down every last logistical detail is, in my view, overdoing things somewhat.

Using the services of a 'fixer' – a local expert who can make arrangements ahead of your arrival – can be useful on occasions. If, for example, you need the permission of indigenous tribes to pass through certain areas, then some assistance is often necessary. In other instances, however, I worry that people miss out on some enlightening aspects of travel by arranging too much before they go. Some of the most enriching encounters I've had with people from other cultures have been when I've humbled myself and asked for help.

In my experience, most people you ask are happy to assist a stranger in need, and experiencing that human kindness first-hand is one of the great rewards of adventuring. It would be a shame to miss out by over-organising things. When you're making preparations ask yourself if the plans you're making need to be arranged from home, or whether it might be more fun (and often cheaper) to take a leap of faith and sort things out on the hoof.

LEARN TO THINK NATURALLY

An Aboriginal Australian friend of mine called Jeremy Donovan once taught me a lesson that has heavily influenced my approach to adventures, and life in general, actually.

Many Aboriginal Australians believe the human being has three brains; the brain in your head, your heart, and your gut.

The biggest and most significant brain is your gut. It's where your being lives at its most essential level and where your feelings originate and where decisions should be made.

The second biggest brain is your heart, which adds the context of emotion to the feeling in your gut.

The third, and least important brain, is the one in your skull. This brain is meant to be an analytical filter for decisions.

Too many of us rely only on our smallest brain to make decisions and that can be a real problem. In extreme situations, particularly when you're isolated from people and places you're familiar with, your head can become a place of conflict. Contrary ideas ping back and forth; you start to second-guess decisions; doubt creeps in. In essence, your brain becomes so twisted and tangled it can't be fixed.

Relying more on your gut – the core of your soul – and less on your mind is something I've tried to incorporate into my life.

A HEAD FOR HEIGHTS

Vertical climbing

Sub-zero temperatures have frozen water inside cracks in the rock face overnight. The frozen water has expanded, putting pressure on the stone.

Now the sun's up, its rays slam directly into the face, raising temperatures by 15 degrees in just 10 minutes. The water quickly melts and the rocks begin to crackle as they shatter. Little by little, that rock face you are about to climb is crumbling.

At the elite end of the sport, climbing is staggeringly dangerous. Add falling boulders, avalanches, sudden weather changes, shredded belay ropes, busted bolts and carabiners to simple human error and the risks keep stacking up.

Don't panic though. For amateurs, with proper preparation and supervision on modest climbs, it's no more dangerous than hiking or piste skiing. Indoor climbing on purpose-built climbing walls is incredibly safe and accidents are rare.

The exhilaration when you reach the top of a big wall and look down upon your achievement will make you want to do it again and again – regardless of whether it's your first or 500th climb.

FREE CLIMB EL CAPITAN, YOSEMITE, CALIFORNIA, USA

DIFFICULTY **★★★★★**
ENDURANCE **★★★**★★
NERVES OF STEEL **★★★★★**

DURATION:	3-6 DAYS (SLEEPING ON THE ROCK FACE)
PERSONNEL:	TWO TO THREE
SKILLSET:	HIGHLY EXPERIENCED CLIMBER (OR GO WITH A GUIDE AFTER TRAINING)
RISKS:	GRAVITY!

USA

YOSEMITE NATIONAL PARK

Native Americans gave it various names including *To-tock-ah-noo-lah,* which means *Captain* or *Rock Chief.* Today, it's simply known as *El Capitan* and it's home to one of the world's most difficult rock climbs.

The smell of fresh pine and campfire smoke fills the air as you enter Yosemite Creek campground. There are signs everywhere warning you to store your food in bear-proof canisters. If you've come from Europe, where most national parks are a little less wild, this is a sobering reminder that you are no longer at the top of the food chain.

Bear attacks are rare and, judging by some photos pinned to the trees, it's more likely your car will be ripped apart if you make the mistake of leaving dinner in your vehicle! But you are not here to worry about bears. Tomorrow, you'll be sleeping on a ledge 500 ft above the valley floor. Bears can climb, but not that well.

Ropes, carabiners and harnesses are strewn everywhere. Sweaty, fit, wiry-looking individuals are exchanging opinions on techniques and routes while poring over maps. Through a clearing you can see it. But it takes several

seconds for you to scan your eyes over the enormous vertical slab of rock from the bottom to the top. Gaining perspective is impossible until you see other climbers in their bivouacs on the face – like ants on a giant tree trunk. All of a sudden, cosying up to a hungry Yogi seems like a better alternative.

CLIMBING'S COLOSSEUM

For Yosemite Valley in California, the description 'awe-inspiring' barely does justice to its splendour. Sculpted by glaciers over millions of years, the forested valley is a mile wide and seven miles long. It's a geological marvel with towering peaks of polished rock that rise vertiginously into the heavens. Its beauty is indescribable. It's also heaven for rock climbers.

The jewel in the crown is a granite monolith with near-vertical faces stretching 3,600 ft up

El Capitan

from the valley floor – three times higher than the Empire State Building. El Capitan. The choice of routes up to the summit is almost endless. Jutting out between El Capitan's southeast and southwest faces, one route quite literally stands out – The Nose.

The route up The Nose follows a series of cracks that snake directly up the tallest part of the wall. When you consider all the factors such as steepness, quality, location and difficulty, it's easy to see why this route is considered by many experts to be the best and most physically challenging rock climb in the world.

El Capitan was considered to be unclimbable until as recently as the 1950s. When Half Dome, the other spectacular granite wall in the valley, was climbed by a rival, a slightly peeved Warren Harding and his team turned their attention to trying to unpick The Nose. Rather than attempting it in a single climb, they borrowed methods used successfully in the Himalayas and attached fixed lines between overnight camps on the climb route. In 1958, after a few failed attempts, they finally made it to the summit to secure their place in history.

As time went on, it became apparent that most faces could be climbed in this traditional style. Some more adventurous climbers began looking for routes up El Capitan that could be free climbed.

Free climbing is rock climbing without aids, using just your hands and feet to make progress up a rock face. The climber doesn't use any other special gear to help them climb apart from climbing shoes. Ropes, bolts and other pieces of equipment are in place only to provide protection in case of a fall.

In 1993, Lynn Hill became the first person to free climb The Nose. It took her three days. She returned a year later and did it again in just 24 hours. This was groundbreaking stuff and a game changer in the climbing world.

WHY ROCK CLIMB?

* Climbing can actually relieve stress. Hundreds of feet up a cliff face, clinging on with two fingers and searching for your next foothold, work and money worries won't be of any concern.

* Climbing can build confidence and perseverance. It can develop problem-solving skills and even improve self-esteem. If you can scale a vertical rock face under your own steam, maybe that speech in front of 100 people isn't such a big deal after all.

* It'll make you incredibly lean and fit – you just can't do any serious climbing if you're carrying weight. You'll build muscle and you'll forget, most of the time, that it's a proper work-out because you're so focussed on the job at hand.

* It's just you versus the rock face. As your confidence, fitness and skills increase, you can set your own challenges and travel the world finding them.

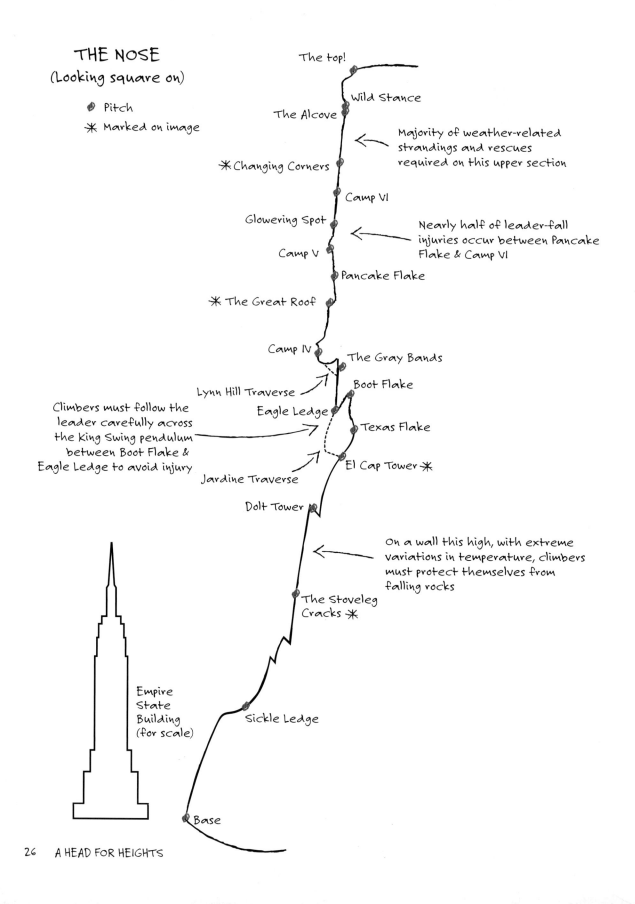

THE NOSE
(Looking square on)

🍃 Pitch
✳ Marked on image

The top!

Wild Stance

The Alcove

Majority of weather-related strandings and rescues required on this upper section

✳ Changing Corners

Camp VI

Glowering Spot

Nearly half of leader-fall injuries occur between Pancake Flake & Camp VI

Camp V

Pancake Flake

✳ The Great Roof

Camp IV

The Gray Bands

Lynn Hill Traverse

Boot Flake

Eagle Ledge

Climbers must follow the leader carefully across the king Swing pendulum between Boot Flake & Eagle Ledge to avoid injury

Texas Flake

El Cap Tower ✳

Jardine Traverse

Dolt Tower

On a wall this high, with extreme variations in temperature, climbers must protect themselves from falling rocks

The Stoveleg Cracks ✳

Empire State Building (for scale)

Sickle Ledge

Base

Changing Corners

The Great Roof

El Cap Tower

The Stoveleg Cracks

DIFFICULTY GRADING

The Nose is rated as a 5.9 C2 VI. What does that mean to those who don't speak rock climbing?

* 5.9 means the climb is technically demanding and/or vertical. It may have overhangs and require specific climbing skills.

* C2 is a reference to the aid required. On a C2 climb, you don't have to hammer in new bolts. You can place your gear and remove it as you go.

* VI refers to the time it takes to ascend the route. VI means a climb of three days or more.

IT'S ALL ABOUT PREPARATION

The Nose is incredibly physically and mentally demanding. It can take up to a week to climb, so the amount of equipment that has to be hauled up the 3,000 ft face is around 100 (highly inconvenient) pounds. No wonder the success rate is so low, both for those who try to free climb it and those who try with aid.

Before you even think about going up The Nose without aid you need to have done multiple big walls with as little aid as possible. Otherwise, you are a fool.

The rocks on El Capitan get baked by the sun and can be almost too hot to touch at certain times of the day in summer. Worse still, the heat also makes them slippery. Those in the know recommend that you complete several practice climbs in California beforehand to get used to the local conditions.

So perhaps do some desert crack climbing to hone those skills. You can then move into the

FREE SOLOING

Free soloing is essentially climbing without any protection whatsoever. No bolts, no rope and nothing to stop a fall. It's pure and incredibly exhilarating but also unbelievably dangerous. One wrong move and it's game over.

Alex Honnold from Sacramento is a pioneer of free soloing. In June 2017 he made it to the top of The Nose without ropes or safety equipment of any kind in just three hours and 56 minutes.

He had this to say: "I go through the same calculation anybody else does with risk taking, is it worth taking the risk? Yes, it is."

Honnold had dreamed of free climbing El Capitan since he was a boy. The climb was years in the planning and he completed dozens of practice ascents at various locations in the US, Europe, Morocco and China to finesse his skills. He did multiple free climbs on The Nose, working out his strategy, before declaring himself ready for the challenge of his life.

Even highly experienced professional climbers have said it's impossible to overstate the physical and mental difficulties involved in a free solo climb of The Nose. Most don't share Honnold's all-or-nothing approach when there is zero margin for error. They have great respect for what he achieved but don't think the rewards match the risks. Put bluntly, if you are a professional free soloer, you can forget about cheap life insurance premiums.

valley and start chalking up the classic routes on Half Dome and the like. These repeated climbs will toughen you up, build your stamina and prepare you mentally.

Climbing The Nose requires you to have a large repertoire of techniques built up over years of experience. What also counts is alpine (i.e. mountaineering) experience – not just having climbed difficult rock faces. You must be comfortable being exposed to the elements at altitude. This means proper mountaineering where you've carried all your food, equipment and shelter as you climb. On The Nose, it's possible to bivouac on natural ledges, which at least means you don't have to cart your bed with you!

Many climbers fail because they can't cope with the exposure over several days. The California sun is relentless – many exhausted climbers are forced to descend as extreme fatigue takes its toll.

ACCIDENTS CAN HAPPEN

Since it was first conquered 60 years ago there have been many accidents and, just to make you feel better, they've been carefully catalogued. More than 40 percent of incidents involve a lead climber falling, often because of problems with the rope anchor points. Bad weather and stranding account for another 25 percent while problems during descent and falling objects also claim a fair share of scalps.

Perhaps surprisingly, one factor that isn't a big problem is inexperience. Many of El Capitan's victims have been highly-skilled climbers with years of mountain time under their belts. Overconfidence can be more dangerous than inexperience.

Climbers pass one danger area with particular caution. Many accidents on The Nose occur between Pancake Flake and Camp VI. The rock face above Camp V is especially treacherous, partly because of the bone-crunching ledges that lie below the more difficult climbs on this pitch and partly because the summit is within sight. Tiredness and even a momentary slip in concentration can be life-threatening as the climb reaches its finale.

TRAIN WITH THE PROS

Luckily for lesser mortals with modest climbing experience, there is an easier and safer way to conquer The Nose. Going with a guide from Yosemite's Mountaineering School and Guide Service means that *relatively* inexperienced climbers who have completed a training course can climb El Capitan.

Don't be lulled into a false sense of security though. Even with a guide and using aids, it's still an incredibly demanding week-long climb. There are no soft options.

You need to be very fit and be able to replenish your energy levels by getting a decent night's sleep – no easy task when there is a 2,000 ft drop beside you. You'll be 'roped in', but this adventure isn't suitable for sleep walkers.

If you can deal with all this, however (and the many, many other challenges), the climb of your life awaits.

MURDER WALL: THE NORTH FACE OF THE EIGER

Shattered Pillar; Difficult Crack; Brittle Ledges; The White Spider; Death Bivouac – even to non-mountaineers, these names conjure up an aura of dread and danger. But to those who know the Eiger mountain, they generate almost primitive feelings of awe and respect.

The Eiger is a 13,020-foot peak in Switzerland. Its north wall (or 'Nordwand') is the largest in the Alps and the most notorious mountain face in the world. This is a vertical mile of crumbling limestone and sheer ice, whipped by howling winds.

It's the first major Alpine peak that any nasty weather system coming from the northwest will meet; while the concave frontage embraces bad weather, holding the storms close to its stone flanks.

In spring, the Eiger starts 'shedding', when regular avalanches of ice, snow and rock tumble down its walls as the mountain shrugs off its winter coat. These deadly cascades are a regular feature of summer afternoons as the air warms. The whole face can seem to be in motion with thunderous waterfalls carrying murderous rocks and shards of ice.

No other great mountain occupies such a public position. In the resort town of Kleine Scheidegg below the North Face, tourists can watch the climbers through telescopes as they inch upwards through the dangers. In the late 1930s a series of tragedies, played out in front of gawping onlookers below, would immortalize the Nordwand and make it irresistible to climbers.

In July 1938, after a hellish climb, two Austrians (Heinrich Harrer and Fritz Kasparek) and two Germans (Anderl Heckmair and Ludwig Vörg), became the first to conquer it. The ascent was an extraordinary technical and athletic achievement that captured the public imagination. Instant worldwide fame awaited their return.

THE EIGER TODAY

The North Face has now been climbed many times, but at least 64 climbers have died on the face since 1935, earning it another nickname – 'Mordwand' ('Murder Wall'). It's still considered to be a formidable climb, commanding the utmost respect, even though modern climbing equipment has made it technically 'easier'.

However, climate change and increasingly erratic weather have reduced the icefields on the face and increased the frequency of rock falls. More climbers are choosing to attempt the North Face in winter when ice helps to strengthen the rock face, but even highly experienced mountaineers remain wary of the world's most notorious climb.

Fortunately, you don't have to be a seasoned climber to experience the North

Face in all its glory. A climbing ladder will take you up the western side of the face. Going with a certified mountain guide, you can reach the 8,737-foot Rotstock Peak. You need to be a fit hiker and have a very good head for heights, obviously.

You'll be roped in for safety, and rock falls are still a risk so don't be fooled into thinking it's easy. It does, however, give the average day hiker a chance to gain some semblance of what it feels like to climb the murderous North Face.

MORE CLIMBING LOCATIONS

TORRES DEL PAINE NATIONAL PARK, CHILE

These wind-whipped peaks in deepest Patagonia look like something from a fantasy movie. Stabbing into the sky, surrounded by glaciers and icefields, the grey walls of stone are enough to set the pulse of any climber racing.

The region's crowning glory is the Torres del Paine National Park, with its three distinctive peaks. Their sheer columns look intimidating and many routes to the summit are the preserve of the best of the best, but a good guide will lead you to ascents which can be tackled by a moderately experienced climber.

The main threat here is wind. Freezing air currents brew in the Antarctic before charging north and blasting into the first solid surface they come across – the mountains you're climbing. It's vital you team up with guides who know the local conditions and how to handle them.

KRABI, THAILAND

This weird but wonderful jumble of limestone cliffs, emerald jungle and turquoise water attracts climbers from all over the world. Scaling vertical faces with the tropical waters of the Andaman Sea hundreds of feet beneath you is a world away from the snow and rock landscapes of the Alps or the Rockies.

The rock here is not to be trusted. The soft limestone is beaten by sea water and monsoon rainstorms, which makes it pretty crumbly – make sure the bolts you've roped to are well secured.

Unlike many popular climbing destinations, Krabi is home to masses of indigenous wildlife. Coming face-to-face with a territorial monkey is a bit different from the usual climbing problems.

Railay Beach,
Krabi Province, Thailand

WHAREPAPA, NORTH ISLAND, NEW ZEALAND

Most climbers who visit New Zealand head for the spectacular peaks of the South Island, but the North Island's crags have a charm all of their own. Rising from a green, pastoral landscape, the cliffs and sheer columns of Wharepapa boast hundreds of routes, ranging from the fairly straightforward to the devilishly difficult.

There aren't a lot of commercial climbing operations here so there's a bit of homework to do before you go, but the laid-back vibe and stunning scenery make the research worth your while.

SURF AND TURF
Sea kayaking and wild camping

It's the end of a long day. Hours of paddling through open seas is starting to take its toll on your body. You notice it most in your fingers, despite the waterproof gloves. They feel as if someone's been going at them with a cheesegrater. The shore is about 30 yards to the right and you're finally within touching distance of that spot on the map that looked like a good place to set up camp. You start heading for dry land when you realize you are not alone.

A huge fin cuts through the surf to your left, accompanied by a spout of water. It's a Volvo-sized orca and it passes right underneath your kayak. Another two or three pop up on either side. Then... too many to count. The pod drifts past, moving fast and with effortless ease. Just as suddenly as they arrived, they're gone. You're buzzing from the sheer thrill of being so close to these graceful giants, but there's no time to dawdle. The sun is setting and you still need to get off the water.

Tonight, when you make camp, you'll have a chance think back on what you've just seen. Maybe you'll catch a glimpse of the Northern Lights before your exhausted body shuts down for the night. And tomorrow you get to do it all again...

THE LOFOTEN ISLANDS, NORWAY

A loop of the Lofoten Islands by sea kayak is an unforgettable experience and the best way to familiarize yourself with the spectacular coastline of Norway. By plotting a route along the scenic shoreline and wild camping overnight, you're submitting yourself to the rhythm of the seas and will learn to appreciate life's simple pleasures.

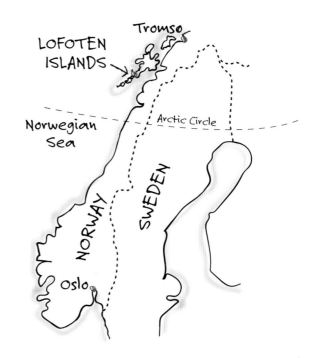

DIFFICULTY **★★★★**★

ENDURANCE **★★★★**★

NERVES OF STEEL **★★★**★★

DURATION: 7–10 DAYS
PERSONNEL: THREE PADDLERS
SKILLSET: EXCELLENT SEA KAYAKING TECHNIQUE, UPPER BODY STRENGTH
RISKS: EXPOSURE, HYPOTHERMIA, DROWNING

The land meets the sea dramatically on the stunning coastline of Norway – a seemingly never-ending succession of dramatic fjords, moody islets and jagged mountain peaks. It's a coastline that stretches for a staggering 15,000 miles, far beyond the Arctic Circle.

It's beautiful, it's rugged and it's just begging to be properly explored. To make the most of Norway's shoreline, you've got to take to the sea. Kayaking the coast gives you a totally unique perspective on one of Earth's natural wonders.

Tackling the whole Norwegian seaboard is a one-of-a-kind, pioneering challenge for the ages. It's also going to take several years out of your life. If you have the guts and the means to make such a commitment – go for it!

For anyone who has to be a bit more frugal with their time, however, there are a mind-boggling number of bite-sized adventures to be had.

Take the Lofoten Archipelago, for instance. This chain of mountainous islands sits way north

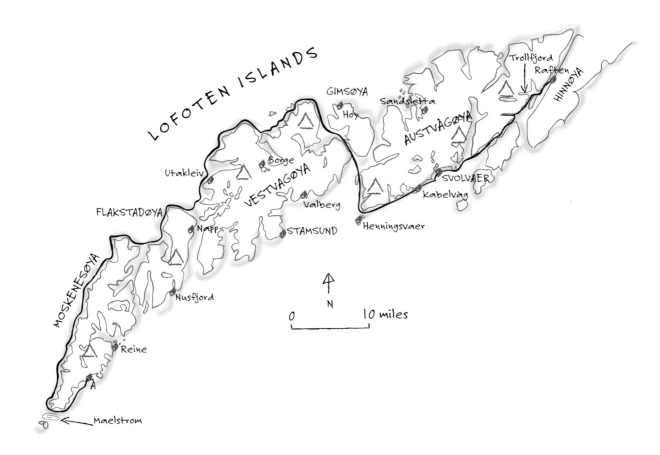

of the Arctic Circle on about the same latitude as Greenland and the Yukon. By all rights, a paddle round here should be chillier than a night in the freezer. It's not, thanks to the Gulf Stream, a huge current of warm water which travels from the Caribbean all the way across the Atlantic Ocean to the west coast of Europe for the sole purpose of keeping you cosier in a kayak.

The islands are like Norway in miniature – a needle-shaped mountain here, a glorious fjord there – and dotted with gorgeous sandy beaches which make for easy landings. Throw in the Norwegian practice of *allemannsretten*, which translates as 'every man's right' and means wild camping is widely permissible (see page 39), and you've got the makings of a proper adventure.

MAKING PLANS

A word of warning – don't scrimp on pre-planning. If you don't get it right before you go, it'll be impossible to rectify the situation when you're on the water. For an expedition of this nature, you'll want to journey with at least a couple of travelling companions. Make sure you team up with people who are committed to the same kind of adventure. There's no point having travel mates who are constantly over the horizon ahead or lagging far behind you. Take a few day-long kayak trips to see how you work together. Be honest with yourself and with each other about how you'll get on.

Get your hands on a *Statkart* map and study it extensively. Make a record of mud flats or tidal shallows, as you'll need to navigate around them. Plot out the most suitable places to overnight and plan your route accordingly; be realistic about how far you'll be able to travel in a day (moderate paddlers should plan on travelling about three miles per hour) and where you will be able to camp discreetly. Take careful note of coastal settlements where you'll be able to replenish your supplies.

You can't do too much checking of maps, tides or weather patterns. Get all these things right before you go and you'll greatly enhance your chances of an unforgettable experience. You'll also reduce the risks.

Being out on the open water when the weather turns is a different kind of scary. You are totally exposed, even if you're no more than a few dozen yards from shore; if a storm hits, it may as well be a million miles.

Always know where your nearest 'safe harbour' is at any point in time. This might be a real harbour or just a sheltered cove somewhere where you can get ashore without playing Russian Roulette with the cliffs. Fortunately, the Lofoten Islands provide lots of options to reach safety.

Check the weather repeatedly before you set off and don't go if you have doubts.

Before tackling the Lofoten Islands, over time you will have become intrinsically aware of your individual capabilities, but experience can be a brutal teacher. Be realistic about your ability to handle heavy winds and strong tides and plan your day's travel accordingly. No matter where you venture out to sea, you must check the tide patterns and plan round them. You'll want to launch when the tide is helping – or at least not hurting – and watch out for conditions when the wind is blowing directly against the tide. You won't enjoy those choppy waves.

MAGNIFICENT MAELSTROM

The concept of a vicious whirlpool that sucks boats into the deep and condemns sailors to a watery grave is a staple of many a nautical yarn. Like a lot of tall stories, it has its roots in fact. The Norwegian word for this natural wonder is 'maelstrom' and the daddy of all maelstroms is found just south of the Lofoten Archipelago.

The Moskstraumen is unlike other whirlpools. First, it's on the open sea, when most are found in rivers or straits. Second, and more importantly, it's huge. In the high summer, when tides are strongest, it spits, gurgles and pulls in water on a frightening scale, tugging at objects up to five miles away.

The maelstrom is caused by warring tides and currents bumping together as they travel in different directions, amplified by sandbars, which make the water unusually shallow. To truly appreciate Moskstraumen you need to get an eagle's eye view. A climb to the summit of nearby Lofotodden, nearly 2,000 feet above the sea, does the job quite nicely.

WILD CAMPING, LOFOTEN ISLANDS

There are few restrictions on wild camping in Norway, thanks to the custom of 'allemennsretten', but there are some guidelines every camper should follow. Basically, they boil down to one simple philosophy – don't be a moron:

* Stay away from people's property (more than 150 metres from houses or cabins, as a rule).

* Get the landowner's permission if you're going to be camping for more than one night.

* Saltwater fishing is fine but only catch what you're going to eat.

* Make sure, when you leave, there is little or no sign that you were ever there.

PADDLES IN

You'll almost certainly find yourself starting your journey on Lofoten's east coast because that's where all the main settlements are. The shallow inlet at Raften, on the island of Hinnoya, is a great place to get going. Heading southwest will take you along fjords so narrow you'll think you can touch both sides with your paddle, and you'll have a chance to explore stunning Trollfjord, maybe with a few massive sea eagles circling overhead. An overnight camp on one of this area's many uninhabited islets sets you up for a second day which takes you into the port of Svolvaer. It's busy round here, so wild camping is going to be tricky, but for one night only why not treat yourself to a decent sleep in a comfortable

Near Reine,
Lofoten Islands

bed and a warm shower before setting off into the wild again?

Head west until you reach the picture-postcard village of Henningsvaer. It's laid out on a cluster of small islands underneath a Toblerone-shaped mountain. Then switch shores by heading north through more narrow fjords on to the increasingly rugged Norwegian Sea coast.

Over the next few days you'll come across some of the finest beaches in Norway – some of the finest beaches anywhere, actually. Go at the right time of year and, with a bit of luck, you might say hello to a pod of orcas too.

Many of the beaches here, such as the majestic sands at Horseid, Bunes and Kvalvika, can't be reached by road. A driftwood fire,

Orcas, Vestfjord, Lofoten Islands

ANIMAL ISLANDS

Full disclosure – if you want an orca encounter like the one described here, you're going to get very cold. These ocean giants only frequent the waters round the Lofoten Islands in the winter months. The Gulf Stream takes the edge off the winter bite but you'll still want to wear more than shorts and a T-shirt. But who cares about a bit of cold when you get a chance to get up close and personal with an orca? They come to this part of Norway for the herring and they're not alone; humpback, minke and fin whales are there for the fishy buffet too.

Whale sightings in summer are far less common, although you might still see minke or the occasional wandering sperm whale, but the midnight sun opens up other possibilities. Sea eagles, with wing spans stretching to seven feet, scour the coastline for a good meal. The sight of an enormous eagle swooping down from on high to snatch its prey from the water is pretty special. The sheer cliffs make great breeding grounds for seabirds like puffins and cormorants, while Eurasian otters are common in many fjords.

a beach to yourselves and a couple of beers after a hard day's paddling – what could be better?

By this point you'll have been paddling for about a week. Your senses will be heightened, your technique will be well-honed... and your body will be screaming for a rest. You can't have one though because the next stage is the toughest test of your adventure so far.

Navigating round the southern point of the island of Moskenesoya takes you within earshot of the notorious Moskstraumen – what the Norwegian's call a maelstrom – one of the world's largest whirlpools (see panel on page 37).

You won't want to get too close to the tides and eddies which make these waters surge but even as you hug the coastline you'll be able to hear its constant roar.

Your journey ends when you glide in to the economically named village of Å. There's not much here, just a couple of shops and a restaurant that caters for cruise liners. If one is in, you can parade around in front of the passengers with a smug satisfaction that comes with getting somewhere under your own steam. You've negotiated a hundred miles of Norway's stunning coast on this trip. Only 14,900 left to explore...

Reine

MORE SEA KAYAKING LOCATIONS

NA PALI COAST, KAUAI, HAWAI'I, USA

Kauai's jaw-droppingly beautiful northwestern coast makes for a magnificent multi-day paddle but it's not for the faint-hearted. First the good stuff. It's rather beautiful here – thousand-foot-high cliffs plunge into clear seas; curious spinner dolphins pop over to greet you as you paddle along; empty beaches with sand like talcum powder and verdant green forests beg to be explored when you get to shore.

Now the bad bits. Actually getting to shore can be tough; negotiating heavy surf takes some skill and lots of muscle. You'll need to bring supplies for the duration of your trip and plenty of water purification tablets. Lastly, exposure to the sun can have you in all sorts of trouble if you're not careful.

If you can overcome those difficulties, one of the world's finest cliff-side kayak tours is yours for the taking.

INSIDE PASSAGE, NORTH AMERICA

The thousand-mile paddle from the Puget Sound in Washington State to Juneau, the capital city of Alaska, is a journey for the ages. The connected network of inlets and straits are sheltered from the worst of the Pacific waves by outlying islands, which makes for outstanding kayak conditions.

Travelling north involves a journey along the rugged Canadian coastline, where there are numerous options to depart from the main channel and explore quiet passages of still waters, before reaching the wilderness of southern Alaska. Along the way you're likely to be accompanied by all sorts of marine mammals, including orcas, seals, dolphins and sea otters. Keep your eyes peeled and you may also spot bears on the shoreline. Best of all, the route fringes Glacier Bay National Park, where huge rivers of ice creep down to the sea. Paddling between floating hunks of ice with a frozen cliff for a backdrop is unforgettable – just don't get too close!

COMOROS ISLANDS, INDIAN OCEAN

These tropical islands, wedged between Mozambique on the African mainland and the island of Madagascar, are perfect for anyone who wants to get off the beaten track. The small island of Moheli has the nation's one and only national park, which includes the spectacular Nioumachoua Islands. The waters round these isles have pristine coral reefs, beautiful sands and a resident population of green turtles, who visit Moheli's beaches throughout the year to lay their eggs.

A visit here can actually do some good, too. By coming to this overlooked patch of paradise, you are supporting community-based ecotourism projects, which in turn fund measures to stop turtle poachers.

WALK IN THE WOODS

Forest hikes

There is something wonderfully random about picking two points that people don't usually travel between – certainly not on foot anyway – and walking from one to the other. It's an adventure for adventure's sake; a deeply personal quest that won't win you bragging rights with others but will teach you so much about your own character. You have to think on your feet, rough it in the wild and learn to keep moving in conditions that wear you down and test your will.

And there's something even better about doing such a mission in the deep woods.

There are no shortcuts or clangingly obvious points of reference to guide your path. Once you're committed, there's no easy way out. Whether you're negotiating rocky ravines in mountain woodland or tackling a claustrophobic jungle, it'll take proper bushcraft and navigational skills to succeed. Nowhere bustles with life like a tropical forest, and during your journey you'll become just another moving part of this massive, heaving cauldron of life.

Plotting a path in the woods is daunting. Imagine trying to find your way on a mountain in dense fog. Or crossing the Arctic in permanent whiteout conditions. That's the scale of the challenge you'll be facing. Get it wrong... well, let's not dwell on that. The best thing about this kind of adventure, though, is the strong possibility that you'll be charting a course where no human has ever been before. Feels a bit special, doesn't it?

AMAZON NATIONAL PARK, FRENCH GUIANA

Plot a route through the pristine Amazonian rainforest of French Guiana, one of the least-visited corners of a part of South America that's not that busy to start with. There's no prescribed route or well-worn circuit set out by other adventurers. You're forging your own path in an untouched hinterland.

DIFFICULTY **★★★★**★
ENDURANCE **★★★★**★
NERVES OF STEEL **★★★**★★

DURATION:	10–14 DAYS
PERSONNEL:	TWO
SKILLSET:	NAVIGATION, BUSHCRAFT
RISKS:	GETTING LOST, TROPICAL ILLNESS

N
0 — 50 miles

Atlantic Ocean

Saint-Laurent-du-Maroni
Kourou
Devil's Island
Saint-Élie
CAYENNE
SURINAME
FRENCH GUIANA
Régina
Maripasoula
Inini
AMAZON NATIONAL PARK
Camopi
BRAZIL

In the top-right corner of South America, quietly minding its own business in a shady spot just above the equator, sits the tiny territory of French Guiana. Covering slightly more than 30,000 square miles, this overseas region of France is about the same size as Austria, but with less than one thirtieth of the population. Nearly all of these people live on the coast, which means there's a massive back garden with hardly anyone in it.

There's a reason most Guianese stick to the coast and you only need a quick look at some satellite imagery to understand this for yourself. French Guiana looks like God has fitted a thick green carpet across the entire place. And when you delve down, into the forest's fabric, you'll find a near impenetrable mass of rainforest that has spent the last few thousand years growing in any direction it damn well pleases.

It's a true wilderness, untouched by humankind, save for a few remote villages hacked out of the jungle and a small number of indigenous tribes who make their home in the heart of the forest.

Walking around trees in F.G. isn't as easy as you might think when the buttress roots are this big

An expedition into this wild country should not be taken lightly. In this environment a walk in the woods can turn into a battle for survival astonishingly quickly.

TEAMING UP

There are all sorts of things you'll need to have in place before you go, not least finding a team-mate to share the journey. You'll need a guide or travelling companion who is as committed to the adventure as you are. It needs to be someone you can get along with, obviously, but you need to be disciplined about how you treat the relationship. A few days of hacking through heavy forest can play all sorts of tricks on your mind. It might sound strange, but the most trivial of things can be blown out of all proportion when you're deep in the journey. Choosing which side of a tree to cut a path round, for instance, is pretty immaterial but it's the kind of thing that starts to play on your mind. Before you know it, you start questioning your travel-mate's decision to go left or right and the whole thing descends into a steaming row. It's essential that you acknowledge this kind of bizarre behaviour is part and parcel of what you're doing. Make sure you're travelling with someone you know can shrug off the manic moments and keep going forward.

You'll need to immerse yourself in the topography of the area as much as you can. Once you're walking on the forest floor, there are very few clues to help you find your way about. There are no crags or hilltops to set yourself against and a thick forest canopy can block out the sun. It's almost like you need X-ray vision. Poring over detailed maps and satellite images can give you an innate feel for the landscape you're hiking through. It'll help you recognize the general lie of the land. Hard study of all the

LOCAL KNOWLEDGE

Cutting-edge kit is all well and good but sometimes it pays to go local. In the Amazon basin, it's important to look after your feet. It turns out the most effective way to wade through water is to get a cheap pair of rubber gumboots and punch a small hole near the base to allow the water to run out. Fancy fishing nets are going to get ripped to shreds by river beasts and you won't be able to fix them when you're miles from civilization. Buy a net when you're out there from someone who uses them every day.

available landscape information – and a good old compass round your neck – will keep you right.

Once you've done all you can to set things up, it's time to head for base camp. The small town of Maripasoula lies roughly 140 miles inland on the border with Suriname and is a decent place to use as 'mission control'. It's accessible by air and river and is a starting point for tourists visiting the nearby Amazon National Park. A few days here, getting your bearings, topping up on basic provisions and harvesting some local information on the surrounding terrain is time well spent.

From here, any journey that takes you east is going to dispatch you into heavy rainforest. Be realistic about how much wild country you want to bite off. Bear in mind that your daily progress may sometimes amount to little more than one kilometre if you're battling through the really heavy stuff.

HOW TO WIELD A MACHETE

Here's a list of things you don't want to happen to you while you're walking in the jungle:

1: Being taken by a caiman.

2: Being bitten by a snake.

3: Hurting yourself with your own machete.

Truth be told, there's not much chance of the first two happening. The third option is a possibility if you don't know what you're doing. Stabbing yourself in the leg or lopping off a fingertip when you're in the middle of nowhere is a situation that's probably best avoided.

With that in mind, here are a few golden rules for using a machete that you should never forget:

1. You are only as sharp as your machete. A blunt blade requires the use of more brute force, which means wilder swings to get through vegetation.

2. Never wear gloves. It may seem like an obvious thing to wear gardening gloves to protect your hands from thorns and blisters but if they slip off you could end up hurling the machete forward - point first.

3. Imagine a 'bubble' around you. Front, rear, left, right - even above you. Never use your machete if anyone is inside or close to your bubble.

4. Don't sharpen the blade next to the handle. From time to time your hand will slip onto the blade, so this portion is never sharpened.

5. Strike wood at 45 degrees, as you would for chopping a log.

A happy-looking black caimen

The Inini River, which heads east from the town into the interior, is a really useful artery for getting you to a start point. Charter a boat to take you upriver for as far as you think you can manage, get out, and begin walking back. Simple!

MEET THE NEIGHBOURS

The rainforest of French Guiana, much of it protected within the Amazon National Park, is one of the last great strongholds of the Amazon jungle. Logging, ranching and mining here is negligible. The diversity of plant and animal life is truly staggering and has to be seen to be believed. For instance, the mighty kapok tree can grow nearly 200 ft tall and has a trunk that is covered in thorns as big as a rhino's horn. Then there are the local residents who might pop in to say hello from time to time. Catching a few fish for your dinner becomes a lot more interesting when a black caiman, which can measure up to 20 ft long, or a giant river otter the size of a

golden retriever come by to see what's on the menu. In these moments, when you're face-to-snout with nature, you truly appreciate how lucky you are to be alone in the woods.

The biggest challenge you'll endure will be the one in your head. The continuous slog of forest navigation will take a toll. It's essential to switch off from time to time. Take turns to navigate and, when it's not your turn, butt out and follow your partner's lead. Allow for a few minutes' rest time every hour and use your GPS for occasional guidance, not as a constant directional tool.

A deep forest walk isn't for everyone. There's no 'hallelujah' moment on top of a summit, no Hollywood views to capture on camera and not much in the way of bragging rights. You're doing this to prove something to yourself, no one else. It's not even about where you start or where you finish. It's the bit in between – the wild, untouched country where no path has ever been forged and no foot has ever fallen – that brings you to your senses.

PAPILLON: ESCAPE FROM DEVIL'S ISLAND

Modern-day French Guiana is a tranquil place but one infamously dark episode casts a shadow on its history. Ask someone if they've heard of the Salvation Islands and most likely all you'll get in return is a blank look. Use their more notorious nickname, however, and it's a whole other story.

Devil's Island (L'Ile du Diable) is actually the title of the smallest of these three dots on the map, which lie about 10 miles from the coastal town of Kourou, but the grisly moniker fitted so well with the brutal Bagne de Cayenne penal colony that it stuck and became known worldwide.

More than 80,000 men were imprisoned on the islands – known as the Green Hell – before they were closed in the 1950s. The conditions were horrendous. Thousands tried to escape but the vast majority died trying.

The most famous escapee was convicted murderer Henri Charrière. He denied the charges and devoted his life to escaping. His exploits were to capture the imagination of millions around the world. His first attempt in a small open boat took him an incredible 1,800 miles to Maracaibo in Venezuela. Unfortunately for Henri he was apprehended while living with native tribespeople and taken back to the islands.

He made seven more attempts to flee before finally escaping for good in 1944 after 13 years' captivity. His autobiography 'Papillon' has sold five million copies in multiple languages and was made into the famous film starring Steve McQueen as the man himself.

Some people think Charrière's stories were exaggerated, to say the least, and several books have vigorously debunked his claims – but the legend of Papillon, Devil's Island and one man's remarkable struggle to free himself from hell on Earth, lives on.

MORE GREAT FOREST WALKING

It's a bit too flippant to say that if you've seen one jungle, you've seen them all, but there's a grain of truth to it. French Guiana's unspoilt nature and (relatively) strong conservation programme make it a great choice for a rainforest walk but there are literally hundreds of other options for an adventure of that type. Pick a place that suits you. If you want to try something different, read on below...

OLYMPIC FOREST, WASHINGTON STATE, USA

For such a wild place, Olympic National Park is ridiculously accessible. It's only a two-hour drive from the urban sprawl of Seattle but almost all hikers stick to the well-maintained designated paths. Take a turn off the trail and you can expect to have a big chunk of these mighty, mountainous woods to yourself for a backcountry adventure.

The park is split in two by the Olympic Mountains and the forest you'll find differs greatly depending on which side of the divide you're on. The sheltered east is dryer. The trees are smaller and the undergrowth less dense than in the west, where clouds rolling in off the Pacific Ocean dump massive loads of water to create the biggest temperate rainforest in the continental United States. Everything here is lush. Moss wraps round trees like a bright green blanket and the going underfoot can be squelchy, to say the least.

Start your journey at the Staircase Campground in the park's less-visited southeast corner and chart a westerly course to the Hoh Campground. It's a journey of about 40 miles as the crow flies. You're not a crow, though, and your route will have to skirt 7,000-foot mountain peaks, traverse steep-sided valleys and cross fast-running rivers. Allow yourself a week to complete the crossing and don't forget to sort a wilderness camping permit before you head out.

It's demanding country, no doubt about that, but the surroundings are awe-inspiring. In the Hoh Rainforest you'll

European Bison,
Białowieża Forest, Poland

find forest giants like the Sitka Spruce (which grows to more than 300 feet), the Douglas-fir and the Western Hemlock Spruce. There's amazing wildlife, too, including cougars, brown bears, bobcats and elk.

BIAŁOWIEŻA FOREST, BELARUS/POLAND

This little patch of eastern Europe is a relic from a different age. An enormous primeval woodland used to cover much of the European plain, stretching hundreds of miles from modern-day France in the west to the Russian steppe in the east. It's gone now. Well, almost gone. The Białowieża Forest is all that remains and this last surviving remnant, roughly 550 square miles in size, is at risk from logging and urbanization. In these woods you'll find ancient species of oak and conifer and Europe's last population of bison.

Unsurprisingly, strenuous efforts are being made to preserve the last remaining woodland. Part of the forest has been declared a UNESCO World Heritage site while other areas are covered by local preservation laws. As a result, you may need a guide to wander through certain parts of the forest. Check before you go. But above all, make sure that you do indeed go, while there's still forest to explore.

WHITE WILDERNESS
Ski tours

You are inching your way up a steep gully that no other human foot in a ski boot – or any other kind of footwear – has ever stepped on. At the top, you will be the first-ever person to stand on the mountain summit. After you have basked in some midnight sun and a little glory, you can ski down the other side at top speed on a snowfield that, again, no human has visited before. It's a thought that humbles you. And thrills you to the bone. This is the moment you came to the frozen end of the earth for.

You crest the knife-edge ridge and your jaw drops open. In front of you the black spine of the ridge continues, a

dagger stabbing between blue-green fjords. Offshore, in the distance, are the icebergs and pack ice of the Greenland Sea. Behind you lies an unexplored snowy gully leading to a thousand lonely miles of ice plateau and beyond that, somewhere, the North Pole. Oh yes, this is the moment. You click the heels of your boots back into their bindings, bring your skis parallel, and drop off the ridge into an absolutely uncharted 45-degree funnel of snow.

KULUSUK, GREENLAND

Ski touring is about getting out into the backcountry, far away from pistes and lifts and après-ski Jagermeister bars. In a ski tour of the vast ice plateau of Greenland your skis will cut the crust of snowfields that have only ever been broken by the paws of wolves and bears. You'll camp at the head of fjords packed with shunting icebergs. This may be the most solitary, humbling – and majestic – experience of your life.

Qaanaaq

GREENLAND

Upernavik

Ittoqqortoormiit H

Uummannaq
H

Qeqertarsuaq
Ilulissat
H
Kangaatsiaq H Qasigiannguit
Sisimiut

Arctic Circle

Maniitsoq
Tasiilaq
H Kulusuk

NUUK

✈ Airport

H Heliport

DIFFICULTY ★★★★★

ENDURANCE ★★★★★

NERVES OF STEEL ★★★★★

Paamiut H
Ivittuut H
Qaqortoq H Narsaq
Nanortalik H

Atlantic
Ocean

N

0   200 miles

DURATION:	AROUND 20 DAYS
PERSONNEL:	GROUP OF FOUR AND GUIDE
SKILLSET:	FITNESS, SKIING EXPERIENCE, WINTER MOUNTAINEERING
RISKS:	AVALANCHE, COLD, EXHAUSTION, POLAR BEARS

Skis – check. Snow shovel – check. Transceiver and probe – check. Plenty of snacks – check.

.338 calibre anti-polar bear rifle with Winchester Magnum cartridges – check. This is skiing all right, but not as you know it.

Few places have as much backcountry skiing as Greenland. This is the largest island in the world and most of it lies inside the Arctic Circle. You could drop Great Britain into Greenland nine times over and still have room for Portugal. A thick ice sheet covers 81 percent of the land, giving you a wintersports wonderland that's more than twice the size of Texas. If this ice sheet melted – and we really hope it doesn't – global sea levels would rise by 23 ft.

Almost all of Greenland's 56,000 inhabitants live on the country's coastal fringe – the hinterland of the island is a mix of sharp rocky mountains, snowfields and vast glaciers. One major advantage of this landscape is that you can step from the seashore pretty much straight onto an Alpine-like playground. Steep, snow-clad peaks climb to over 6,500 ft in no time at all. So you have lots of gnarly crags to climb and couloirs – narrow, steep-sided valleys – to ski down but no pesky altitude sickness to put a handbrake on your happiness.

To get here, it won't be your standard bargain flight and bus ride. The usual route is to fly to Iceland and then hop over the icy Arctic Ocean to the southeastern Greenland town of Kulusuk. Here you can pick up a guide or book a trip with a local company. It's essential to go with someone who knows the area – no matter how much backcountry skiing you have done, you won't have travelled in a landscape quite like this one. Your host company can put you up,

hire your kit and cooking equipment, sort out food and help you put together an itinerary. This will be very much dependent on your skills and fitness, your budget and the whims of Greenland's weather.

One of your most useful bits of kit will be your satellite communication system – not so much for calling home but for checking daily weather forecasts. Storms can be savage here and they can brew up in a heartbeat. Sometimes a stable high pressure system with rising temperatures can be an even more deadly enemy; in a few hours it can destabilize slabs of snow and create avalanches-in-waiting. Avalanches are more common in the late afternoon when the sun has warmed the snow.

They are just some of the dangers you'll face every day. Sheer drops. Uncharted crevasses. Shifting sea ice in the fjords. Intense cold. The shocking remoteness of the place. The lack of any emergency rescue services. There is also the rare but very real threat of being approached by an inquisitive polar bear, so your party will carry flares and a rifle, and if you camp it's wise to set up trip wires around your tents.

Kulusuk

A LIFE OF UPS & DOWNS

Ski touring combines the usual downhill skiing you do in a resort with ski mountain-eering. Ski up, ski down. How come you don't slide back down into the valley? This is where skins come in. These long strips of nylon or mohair fit onto the bottom of your skis. They have a nap, so can glide smoothly forward but their hairs or bristles dig in to the snow to stop you going backwards. The first pairs were made of sealskin, hence the name.

You can slip your skins on standard Alpine downhill skis, but you will need special bindings that can unclip at the back to let you 'free heel'. When skiing along level ground, you unclip your heel and walk using a sort of sliding, gliding forward step. When going up a slope you use heel lifters, little plastic ledges that hold the heel of your boot at an angle above the ski. So your feet stay flat as you climb up the slope on your skis – a surreal but very satisfying way to climb a snowy slope. If the slope is icy, you can also deploy ski crampons for extra bite.

When the slope is super steep, you climb in zigzags across it, using kick-turns to switch direction. You have to watch out for overhanging cornices or angled slabs that could cause an avalanche. If the gradient increases any more it'll be time to strap the skis to your backpack, pull on your crampons and start cutting steps with your ice axes. This is hard, hard work.

All you need is an airport, snow, your skis, and you're ready to make up your own ski touring adventure. In this case, the airport is at Kulusuk.

THE SOUNDS OF SILENCE

To balance out the dangers, you'll benefit from the restorative power of a little quietness. And, apart from the occasional shriek of a seabird and the restless, whistling wind, there is an awful lot of that here. In fact, the sense of solitude can be almost overwhelming. Luckily on many evenings you'll be able to enjoy the local free entertainment. Settle down in camp and get ready for nature to put on one of her most spectacular shows – the Northern Lights. As greens and purples surge and ripple against the icing sugar backdrop of the Milky Way you may find yourself staying well up past your bedtime. Its beauties are more addictive than any TV box set.

BREAKING VIRGIN TRAILS

Finally, and perhaps most importantly, there are the thrills. Ski lifts and cable cars don't exist here, but if you want to get deep into the unknown, you can catch a different sort of ride – a tow from a snowmobile. Being pulled at 30 miles per hour on your skis along the sea ice of a fjord is a terrific way to start the day.

It won't take too much travelling before you find yourself staring up at unclimbed peaks and unskied slopes. There are guides who have worked in Greenland for 20 years and they have barely scratched the surface of one corner of the adventures that this amazing place has to offer. Here you can travel hundreds of miles without seeing another human soul.

In a landscape where no one has ever skied before, you can expect plenty of pristine powder. But there will be so much that you can't possibly predict. A stunning couloir catches your eye – how steep will it be when you get into it? You can't tell for sure – remember, no one has been up it before. But there is snow on it so the face can't be completely sheer. Time to find out...

MULTI-DAY SKI TOURING

THE HAUTE ROUTE, CHAMONIX TO ZERMATT, FRANCE & SWITZERLAND

This most famous and historic ski tour in the Alps crosses massive glaciers and high passes between two of Europe's iconic ski resorts. It takes five or six days with a choice of routes – some of which extend the tour by a few days. You'll ski among the highest and most majestic peaks in the Alps and overnight in spectacularly located mountain huts along the way.

In the mid-section, the easier and more popular route is through the Verbier area. If you fancy a stiffer challenge choose the Valsoray detour, but you'll need to wait for decent weather and stable snow conditions to cross the tricky Plateau du Couloir.

The Haute Route is for very fit and experienced skiers only as it involves tough ascents of around 3,500 feet each day. The effort is well worth it as you make your way across the roof of Europe. The pièce de résistance is the final descent into Zermatt below the Matterhorn's north face.

WAPTA SKI TRAVERSE, CANADIAN ROCKIES, BANFF NATIONAL PARK, CANADA

One of the best hut-to-hut ski tours North America has to offer, this five-day adventure takes you through the Wapta and Waputik Icefields. The route starts at Peyto Lake, not far from the Icefields Parkway road, before heading up into the high country and along the continental divide. The traverse ends near to the Kicking Horse Pass on the Trans-Canada Highway.

Stubai Alps, Austrian Tyrol

"Isolation forces you to come face-to-face with a very raw version of yourself. It's like a mirror to your soul. It can be absolutely terrifying."

FROZEN WATER

Cold-water swims

You hit the water and experience a High Impact Moment. You gasp for breath. Your mouth is desperately trying to inhale, but your lungs haven't got the memo – the effect of ice water hitting skin is literally stunning. Your chest feels like it's been locked in a vice; your arms and legs are waggling away as if you're a puppet and a hyperactive toddler is pulling the strings. This is what a shock to the system feels like.

Then suddenly – beautifully – you're hit by an immense surge of energy. Your lungs fill and your arms and legs fall back into order. The human body is a wonderful thing. Your brain has recognized that you're in a bit of trouble and dispatched a huge wave of adrenalin to flow through your limbs and restore some balance.

It's still bloody cold, of course, but you can live with it – for now – and get on with your plans. After all, you're here to have some fun...

LAKE BAIKAL, SOUTHERN SIBERIA, RUSSIA

Plunge into a world of extreme cold for a challenge of endurance that will take your body to the brink. The strangely addictive pursuit of taking a swim through bone-chilling water is becoming increasingly popular as more and more people swear by its health-giving benefits.

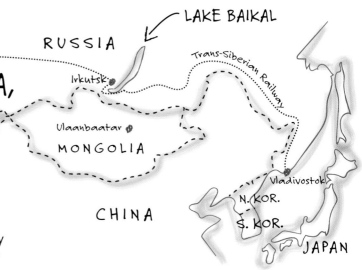

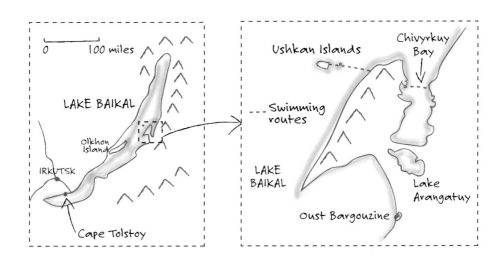

DIFFICULTY ★☆☆☆☆

ENDURANCE ★★★☆☆

NERVES OF STEEL ★★★★☆

DURATION: 2–4 HOURS

PERSONNEL: JUST YOU

SKILLSET: EXPERIENCED OPEN WATER SWIMMER

RISKS: HYPOTHERMIA, LEADING TO DISORIENTATION AND HEART FAILURE!!

We all know using 'unique' to describe a famous landmark is tiresomely overused. In actual fact there are very few places that properly deserve that accolade. So it's no small thing to say that Lake Baikal is unique.

It's the world's biggest body of fresh water (5,500 cubic miles). It's the world's deepest lake (5,315 ft), and its oldest (25 million years old, give-or-take a millennium or two). Someone's actually worked out that if the rest of Earth's supply of drinking water ran out, there would be

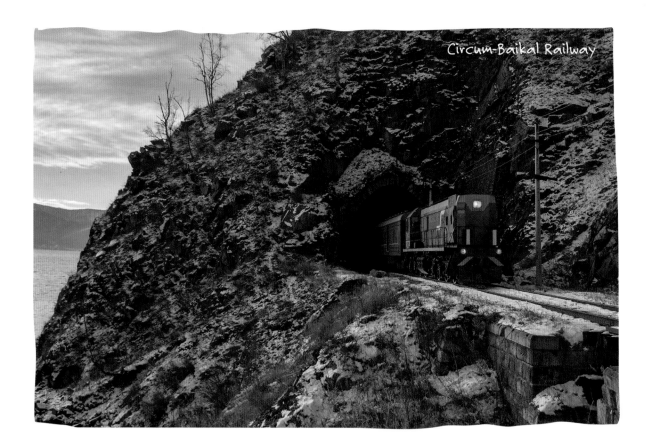

Circum-Baikal Railway

enough of the stuff in Lake Baikal to whet the whistle of all humanity for nearly 50 years.

Lake Baikal's remote location – hidden in the sheer vastness of Siberia – adds to the mystique. So does the spectacular scenery that surrounds its shores. The lake is 395 miles long, shoe-horned between mountain ranges and flanked by steep cliffs and untouched forests.

Then there's the wildlife. According to the World Wildlife Federation, the Lake Baikal area is home to around 2,000 species of plants and animals and a staggering two thirds of them cannot be found anywhere else on Earth. For example, it's home to the world's only species of exclusively freshwater seal. Known as the *nerpa*, its nearest relative is the Arctic ringed seal which lives more than 2,000 miles away. Nobody knows for sure how these sea mammals made

it over mountains, through forests and across plains to Lake Baikal, but about 80,000 of the little rascals live around its waters.

Getting to this wilderness doesn't have to be an adventure in itself. The city of Irkutsk has an international airport and is only a bus ride away. But, as always, what's life without a bit of adventure? The legendary Trans-Siberian Railway stops right on the shore in the town of Slyudyanka. The five-day journey from Moscow is one of the world's great railway experiences and gives you a chance to appreciate the epic expanse of the Russian hinterland.

An extended journey also gives you time to get your mind straight for the challenge ahead because, when you get to the lake, you're going to take a swim. A very, very cold swim.

THE COLD WAR

Visiting Lake Baikal isn't just a chance to take in this unique – yes, unique – landscape. It's also an opportunity to follow in the flippers of one of the world's greatest cold-water swimmers.

When a 32-year-old American called Lynne Cox stood on the banks of Lake Baikal in the summer of 1988, she had already established herself as a pioneer in her chosen field. She'd swum the English Channel in record time – twice – and was the first person to swim between the North and South islands of New Zealand, and across the notoriously boisterous Strait of Magellan in Chile.

A year before her visit to Siberia, Cox had captured worldwide attention by swimming from the United States to Russia. The two-hour-five-minute swim across the Bering Strait, from Little Diomede in Alaska to Big Diomede in the former Soviet Union, earned plaudits from around the world including commendations from US president Ronald Reagan and Soviet premier Mikhail Gorbachev. Now she was to add another milestone to her list of achievements by undertaking a 10-mile swim in the lake's ice-cold waters.

Cox's chosen route along a stretch of the southwest shore measured seven miles as the crow flies but was nearer 10 in the water due to currents.

No one had ever attempted a swim of such length in Lake Baikal. The water temperature at the time of Cox's attempt – even in the summer month of August – was recorded at an extremely bracing 55°F (12.5°C). Given that hypothermia sets in when body temperature dips below 95°F (35°C) it's easy to see why spending several hours splashing about in there could be a bit risky. Nevertheless, Cox completed her challenge in just over four hours and climbed out of the water with a huge grin on her face. More than 3,000 locals stood on the banks of the lake to watch her in action.

Lake Baikal seals or 'nerpas', as they prefer to be known! Ushkan Islands

Olkhon Island

It's usually late June
before all the ice on
the lake has melted.

THE CHILL DRILL – COLD-WATER SWIMMING TIPS

* Double cap: Top your body with not one but two neoprene caps to create a thin layer of air which captures warmth.

* Plug up: Ears are one of the reasons your head leaks heat. Stick in a pair of plugs to cut your losses.

* Shock treatment: Practise getting into cold water. The shock takes some getting used to so see how it feels before you do it for real.

* Warm up well: Your muscles are going to contract in a hurry when you hit cold water. Make sure you're properly stretched before you dive in or something might go snap.

Ice bath, Russian style on Lake Baikal (plus vodka)

THE BENEFITS

As well as being an elite open water athlete, Cox was a big believer in the mental and physical benefits of cold-water swimming. Proper exposure to the cold starts a cascade of health benefits; studies show it increases your metabolic rate, improves your circulation and boosts your immune system.

It also makes you feel good. Many scientists believe plunging into ultra-cold waters prompts your brain to release a big batch of endorphins into your body, which elevates your mood. And a study by scientists at Eastern Washington University found that sitting in water of 55°F for 15 minutes decreases your heart rate which in turn reduces blood pressure and has a calming effect on your body's nervous system.

It's possible to retrace Cox's route for a swim of your own but, truth be told, it's probably not the most enticing option. Cox set out from Cape Tolstoy and swam east across Listvenichny Bay and the mouth of the Angara River to an end point near the town of Listvyanka. It's a challenging stretch to tackle (Cox had to struggle every inch of the way against strong currents) but it's not the most picturesque spot. Why come all this way to settle for anything less than the best?

There's more appealing and clearer water to be found further north, where the lake is quieter and the scenery is wilder. Chivirkuysky Bay, around 300 miles north of Listvyanka, is surrounded by tree-covered mountains, which provide some shelter from the worst excesses of the weather and create a stunning setting for your adventure. A swim across the mouth

QUEEN OF COLD-WATER: LYNNE COX'S GREATEST SWIMS

Lynne Cox started smashing open water records at a young age – and just kept smashing them. She became the youngest person to swim the 27-mile Catalina Channel off the coast of California at the age of 14. A year later she broke the world record for swimming the English Channel – a further year later she went back and broke it again.

Cox spent the rest of the 1970s doing all sorts of ridiculous stuff. In addition to her escapades in New Zealand and Chile, she set a new record for crossing the Öresund between Denmark and Sweden; she became the first person to swim between three islands in the Aleutian Archipelago off Alaska and swam round the shark-infested Cape of Good Hope in South Africa.

After her visit to Lake Baikal, Cox continued to push the boundaries of what was considered possible in freezing water. In 2002 she visited Polar waters and swam 1.2 miles in frozen waters off the coast of the Antarctic Peninsula. It took months for the feeling to return to her hands and feet.

of the bay will measure between five and eight miles, depending on the line you take. The water here is shallower and a bit warmer than in the open lake and you can even round off your swim with a dip in the warm waters of some nearby thermal pools.

If that sounds just a bit too gentle, you can leave the tranquillity of the bay and get into deep water with a crossing from Holy Nose Peninsula to Big Ushkan Island – the stronghold of the nerpa. The Ushkan Islands are a nature reserve and you'll need special permission to make landfall, but the feeling of isolation as you negotiate this 3,000-ft deep passage is something special. Just you, the waves, maybe a bold nerpa... and of course a boat with a support crew following your path because, after all, you are swimming in a near-freezing lake in Siberia.

You might be crazy but you're not an idiot.

Ogoy Island, Lake Baikal
in winter

IN THE CLEAR

Lake Baikal is renowned for its pure water. There's no soupiness here and the clarity that lets you see way into the deep adds to the slightly otherworldly feel of the place. In summer, when filled with melted ice water from the surrounding mountains, visibility can reach more than 600 feet. With a pair of binoculars, it's possible to watch shoals of fish swimming along the lake bed from a vantage point high on the shore.

Why is the water so see-through? The purity of the ice water is one factor, the lack of minerals floating around is another. Uniquely (there's that word again) among deepwater lakes, Baikal's depths are heavily oxygenated, which also contributes to the crystal clearness.

MORE HEART-STOPPING SWIMS

THE LOONIE DOOK, EDINBURGH, UK

Scotland likes to welcome in each new year with the mother of all parties. The country is famous for its Hogmanay celebrations and nowhere more so than the nation's capital city, Edinburgh. The festivities last for three days with more than 80,000 revellers packing the city streets to see in the new year with song, dance and maybe one or two small whiskies to ward off the chill. It's a riotous celebration. And what better way to recover on the morning after the night before than with a quick dip in the sea?

On the morning of New Year's Day, hundreds of revellers head to the outskirts of the city and, in the shadow of the iconic Forth Bridge, take part in the Loonie Dook. The waters of the Forth estuary aren't exactly welcoming but it's certainly refreshing.

WORLD WINTER SWIMMING CHAMPIONSHIPS

If you fancy adding a competitive edge to your cold-water swimming, or just want to mingle with lots of like-minded people, the World Winter Swimming Championships could be just the thing for you.

The first championships, held in Helsinki, Finland, attracted 500 competitors. Since then the event has grown in popularity and more than 1,200 swimmers took part in the 11th championships in the Estonian city of Tallinn in 2018.

Competitive events are held in age-group categories and swum over various distances, from 25 metres to 425 metres. There are also untimed swims for people who just fancy a paddle without the pressure of racing.

There are strictly enforced rules about the amount of time a swimmer can spend underwater, but the emphasis is on enjoyable competition and inspiring people to join in the fun.

SOUTH GEORGIA, ANTARCTICA

Okay, this one is definitely out there but a venture into the frozen waters of the Southern Ocean is pretty cool in every sense of the word. The combination of clear, unpolluted waters and curious wildlife (that hasn't yet realized what utter bastards human beings can be) makes for an unforgettable experience. It's not quite out of this world but it's pretty close.

A few intrepid trailblazers have shown what can be done. Lewis Pugh, a former lawyer from the United Kingdom, swam a full kilometre in waters off the coast of South Georgia wearing nothing but Speedos, goggles and a swim cap to raise awareness of the impact of global warming. It took him 19 minutes and he finished near the grave of legendary Polar explorer Ernest Shackleton.

Lewis Pugh has swum in many locations around the world to raise concerns about our impact on the environment. Here he is in Svalbard. (Courtesy lewispugh.com)

LIFE CYCLE
Long distance bike rides

A long-distance cycle expedition is a great way to strike a balance between making progress and filling your senses.

Journeys by car are too fast; four wheels gives you flexibility and comfort but doors and a windscreen seal you off from your surroundings, and you move at such speed it's often a case of here today, gone tomorrow. Long walks can sometimes be too slow; over time the sheer physical exertion and the plodding rate of progress can wear you down so that you become fixated on your end destination and don't take time to stop and sniff the flowers.

Moving by bike, however, is just right; you can travel at a decent pace but still have time to soak up the view. You'll have a connection with the environment around you but also be able to rack up the miles needed to give your expedition some forward momentum.

Do it right and it's a fairly safe bet that you'll get a taste for it. An incredible number of people who complete one cycling mega-mission immediately start planning their next one. For some, the lure of the open road becomes irresistible and the bike more or less becomes the only home they want – or need.

THE INDIAN SUBCONTINENT

Plunge wheels-first into the mad, mystical, majestic Indian subcontinent for a journey through fascinating cultures and dramatic landscapes. Cycling north from the steamy southern highlands, this bike tour will immerse you in the sights, sounds and smells of Indian life.

DIFFICULTY **★★**★★★
ENDURANCE **★★★★**★
NERVES OF STEEL **★★**★★★

DURATION: THE MORE TIME THE BETTER – NO LESS THAN 3 MONTHS

PERSONNEL: JUST YOU

SKILLSET: BIKE REPAIR, PHYSICAL FITNESS

RISKS: STOMACH PROBLEMS, MAD MOTORISTS

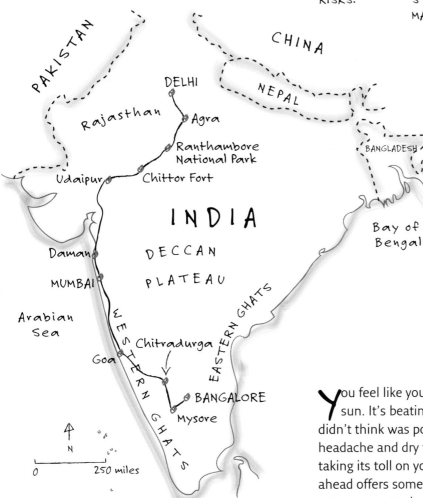

PAKISTAN

CHINA

DELHI

NEPAL

Rajasthan

Agra

Ranthambore National Park

BANGLADESH

Udaipur

Chittor Fort

INDIA

Bay of Bengal

DECCAN

Daman

PLATEAU

MUMBAI

Arabian Sea

WESTERN GHATS

EASTERN GHATS

Chitradurga

Goa

BANGALORE

Mysore

N

0   250 miles

Indian Ocean

Y ou feel like you're under attack from the sun. It's beating down with a ferocity you didn't think was possible and your throbbing headache and dry throat are clear signs that it's taking its toll on you. A small copse of trees up ahead offers some shade, so you decide to stop, get some water in you and stay out of the solar onslaught for a few minutes.

This looked like a quiet stretch of road but no sooner have your feet touched the ground than a throng of interested passers-by flock to your side:

"Where have you come from?... Where are you going to? ... Where did you get your bike? What are you doing here?"

You're pretty knackered and fob off the questions with a shrug and a smile. But if you had the energy and the inclination to respond, your answers would have been: "South. North. Bangalore. And..." well, actually, that last question is a tough one to answer.

You've been cycling for more than 800 miles. There's another 800 to go until you reach your planned destination. Then, after that, who knows? Where are you going? You're going where the path leads you and accepting the truth of that simple answer is both daunting and exhilarating.

LAND OF OPPORTUNITY

India is a travel destination on such a grand scale that planning any kind of big adventure can really frazzle your mind. From the mountain splendour of the Himalaya in the north to the lazy backwaters of Kerala in the south, the breadth of options is dazzling – and confusing.

Picking a route comes down to individual preference and in this day and age there's a wealth of online resources to help with planning. You'll want to travel during the dry season (between October and March), avoid the busiest roads where possible and incorporate a range of cultures and landscapes. Your path should keep you clear of big cities (with the odd exception), where negotiating chaotic traffic is often a contact sport, but be close enough to civilization to allow you to incorporate some rest and recu-

peration and, to be blunt, somewhere to hole up if you can't trust your stomach for a few days.

One of the grandest of grand cycle tours is the long, sweeping northward arc which starts at Bangalore in the south, heads northwest through sumptuous Goa and hectic Mumbai before heading uphill and inland through Rajasthan to Delhi. It's a journey of more than 1,600 miles, and you'll need to allow at least three months to do it justice.

The southern city of Bangalore (Bengaluru) is a decent place to start. With a population of more

Goa

than eight million souls it's the country's third biggest city, and not particularly bike-friendly in itself, but it has excellent transport links and plenty of places to stock up on supplies and make any modifications to your bike. It's also 3,000 ft above sea level, so the journey gets off to a nice, easy, downhill start!

Truth be told, the first section of your epic ride is also one of the dullest. The road to Mysore is 100 miles of nondescript countryside. A glass-half-full type of person would say it gives the perfect conditions to road-test your bike and make sure it is properly set up for the challenges ahead. Even so, it's a relief to reach Mysore. With its ancient buildings and bustling market, it feels like the start of your adventure. It's also a staging point for your first plunge into proper countryside. You'll follow quiet roads to the coastal province of Goa, past paddy fields, coffee plantations, historic buildings and lush forests. Take some downtime to visit and explore the stunning Military Fort at Chitradurga.

BIKE BASICS

The best bike for a long distance tour is the bike you don't have to worry about. That means you're looking for something sturdy that won't be unbalanced when fully-loaded and that can be easily repaired on the hoof.

Be sensible about your bike choice. Are those cutting-edge carbon forks going to be easy to replace if they snap on you in the back of beyond? Give serious consideration to buying a bike at your starting point rather than bringing one from home – parts will be easier to come by and repairs should be more straightforward. If you do bring a bike, include enough essential spare parts to ensure you can always keep the show on the road; inner tubes, a pump, cables, brake pads and spokes. And, whatever you do, make sure you give your rear end the saddle it deserves.

High quality waterproof panniers may seem like an extravagance if you're travelling to a hot, dry country but they don't just keep the wet out, they also stop dust from getting into your gear.

As for the rest... you'll find it liberating taking only what you need and leaving all the non-essential stuff behind. It's a statement about how you're going to live on the road.

Peace and quiet in rural India
between its bustling cities,
interrupted only by a touring cyclist!

THE GOOD GUTS GUIDE

Many, make that most (okay, make that all) travellers who spend months in India have stomach problems during their visit. You're probably expecting a list of 'dos and don'ts' here, which will keep your guts incident free during your bike expedition. Dream on.

Ask a thousand India veterans for their tummy trouble tips and you'll get a thousand different answers. Stick to a few basic rules, however, and you'll reduce your risk of suffering:

* You can't wash your hands too often.

* Steer clear of 'fresh' fruit juice and ice cubes at cafes and restaurants.

* Only buy canned drinks from vendors.

* Don't be scared of street food but keep it sauce-free.

It's probably best to treat a stormy stomach as an intrinsic part of your adventure. Not a fun part, granted, but a part nonetheless. Get all your jabs before you go and allow enough slack on your schedule so that, if calamity strikes, you can take a couple of days off the road and on the john. And don't be a martyr to your schedule by trying to push on when you're weak. Cycling in searing heat when you are dehydrated through illness is just stupid.

Mumbai on a quiet day!

COASTING ALONG

After several weeks of quiet back roads and country living, Goa's garish coastal resorts can come as a bit of a culture shock, but they're full of good value places to stay where you can recharge your batteries before turning north on the next leg of the challenge. You're heading for Mumbai, one of the world's great megacities but probably also one of the most challenging to get across on a bike. You'll be competing for space on crowded streets with 12 million residents – sometimes it feels like they're all using the same bit of road as you – and the cost of living here is noticeably higher than you'll have experienced so far. Best get through it sharply and back to the road less travelled.

Pressing on north takes you through the former Portuguese colonial port of Daman, which is well worth a look round. It's also a point which brings about a big change in your journey. You've been following the coast, keeping the Arabian Sea to your left, for the last 500 miles or so. Now the route heads inland, through bone-dry eastern Gujarat and into Rajasthan.

You're on the road to Udaipur, where the countryside is greener and the temperatures slightly less punishing. At this point, the

Chittor Fort
(or Chittorgarh Fort)

TOP TIPS

Bicycling through India is a riot of noises, sights and sounds. You'll adjust to the country's, erm, 'vibrant' traffic as you rack up the miles but Dibin Devassy, of Indian cycle tour specialists The Art of Bicycle Trips, has a few tips to get you started:

* Don't expect everyone to follow the rules of the road, particularly in cities and big towns, where there are no cycle lanes as such.

* When turning right across traffic, we advise cyclists to dismount, check both ways, and cross on foot.

* Indian drivers honk their horns a lot. They're not being rude. It's just to inform the rider that a vehicle's approaching and will pass by.

* Dress appropriately. India is a vast, rural country and people in villages, who have a traditional way of life, will stare if you expose too much skin. We advise cyclists to cover their shoulders and wear shorts close to knee-length. Bright colours help for visibility, too.

* Dogs can be a problem. If one chases you, and you can't outride it, stop cycling and walk out of the animal's territory. Keep the bike between you and the dog.

* Always ask permission before taking pictures of people.

* Take off footwear before entering someone's home.

compulsion to press on and finish your journey conflicts with the temptation to take a few detours to remarkable sights. No matter how much of a rush you're in, however, there are a couple of landmarks it would be criminal to cycle past.

The incredible Chittor Fort complex is one of Rajasthan's six ancient hill forts and has to be seen to be believed. The scale is just over-whelming. Laid out over nearly 700 acres, and the result of 12 centuries of work, it incorporates temples, towers and palaces of exquisite beauty from a period of history about which many western visitors know shamefully little.

TIGER TRACKS

A few days' journey to the northeast will take you to Ranthambore – the one place on the entire trip where you'll have to ditch the bike for a few days. The Ranthambore National Park is compact in size but it's special because of the resident population of Bengal Tigers who call it home. It's one of the best – and sadly last – places on Earth where the world's biggest cat can be seen in its natural environment.

Your odyssey finishes as it started; with a long slog through many forgettable miles, on the outer orbit of a massive city. Delhi is the end. If you've done nothing but cycle hard every day, you'll have completed the journey in a couple of months. You'll probably also have missed the point. No country on Earth is better suited to unexpected detours, or to turning an overnight stop into a week-long stay. Give yourself time to breathe, to feed your mind with everything India has to offer, and your cycle adventure will be the ride of your life.

PEDAL POWER – OTHER GREAT CYCLES

NEW ZEALAND

The South Island is an absolute paradise for a big, long bicycle ride. The Southern Alps form a backbone for pretty much the island's entire length. Cycling between them on lofty passes will dazzle your eyes – and burst your lungs – but there's so much more to see as well. The northern reaches have golden beaches and beautiful bays, the west coast has forests and glaciers and the spectacular south is all milky blue lakes and jagged peaks. Highlights include snaking through the remarkable Haast Pass and taking the tough but rewarding Molesworth Road between Christchurch and Blenheim. Then there's cruising through Marlborough's wine country, skirting the roaring rivers around Wanaka and Queenstown, peddling past the breakers on the stunning Catlins Coast… your options are almost endless. Wherever you choose to go, you'll find quiet roads in good condition and well-kept hostels and campsites to rest your tired legs.

JAVA

Bike-friendly New Zealand extends a VIP welcome to cyclists (see above) but Java is more of a 'nice to see you, but just get on with it' kind of destination. Crossing Indonesia's most populous island is a rough and ready expedition – a bear of a challenge even for experienced cycle tourers. A string of volcanoes, many of them still active, loom over the entire island. You'll pedal close enough to some of them to smell the sulphur and (almost) hear the lava boiling. In between there are pristine beaches, ancient ruins, verdant jungles and welcoming villages to explore on your 1,100-mile odyssey.

MADAGASCAR

Mention Madagascar and the first thing that springs to mind is probably green forests filled with cute lemurs. Or, if you've got kids, the cartoon movies. The forest stuff is only part of the story, though. The world's fourth-biggest island also boasts stunning highland scenery, which lends itself beautifully to a bike-bound adventure. Throw in all sorts of natural phenomena that you won't find anywhere else – including lemurs – and you've got the perfect backdrop for an unforgettable journey.

Madagascar

ON A KNIFE EDGE

Ridge walks

The drop on your left is 500 feet. On your right it's easily double that. If you stumble and fall, you'll have plenty of time to ponder what went wrong before smashing into a hundred pieces on the solid stone floor below.

In front of you is a rocky spine, no more than six inches across in some places, but room enough to accommodate a well-placed boot - so long as you put it in the right spot.

This narrow ridge is your lifeline. It will take you from mountain top to mountain top through some of the most spectacular scenery on Earth. When you reach the summits you'll have time to stop and drink in the incredible views, but there's a time and a place for sightseeing and it isn't while you're walking the ridge.

This experience will – literally – take you right to the edge. You are focused entirely on the present – there's no room in your head for doubt, or reflection, or worry about the future because every step you take is vital. It's the kind of pure enjoyment you can only get when you test yourself in extreme conditions, one step at a time.

SKYE SCOTLAND

THE CUILLIN RIDGE TRAVERSE, ISLE OF SKYE, SCOTLAND, UK

A demanding scramble along a succession of summits amid some of the most spectacular wilderness in Europe. It's only a few miles from start to finish but every move on the ridge demands attention.

DIFFICULTY **★★★**★★

ENDURANCE **★★**★★★

NERVES OF STEEL **★★★★**★

DURATION:	2 DAYS
PERSONNEL:	MINIMUM TWO PEOPLE (GUIDE ADVISED)
SKILLSET:	ROUTE-FINDING, NAVIGATION, ROPE-WORK
RISKS:	SHEER CLIFF FACES, GALE-FORCE WINDS, SUDDEN DROPS IN TEMPERATURE, VISIBILITY

The Isle of Skye is a wild and rugged island sitting off the west coast of Scotland. You might recognize it, even if you've never been there; the island's otherworldly landscapes feature in big budget Hollywood movies including *Prometheus*, *Snow White and the Huntsman* and *The BFG*.

For centuries these mountains have inspired painters, poets and authors to try and do justice to their beauty. Peaks rise dramatically from the sea, creating a jagged horizon of weird and wonderful shapes on the skyline. It's not just a pretty place, though, it's one of the most dangerous playgrounds in Europe. The Cuillin mountain range, which runs through the heart

of Skye like a backbone of solid rock, may be gorgeous to look at but its steep slopes are no cakewalk.

The toughest challenge of all is the Cuillin Ridge, a trail which links several of the range's highest summits. The raw statistics don't look too daunting. The highest peak, Sgurr Alasdair, measures just 3,255 ft which is not even one quarter the height of a Matterhorn or an Eiger and positively titchy in comparison to some of the monster peaks of the Himalaya.

The Summer Traverse, the most popular route across the ridge, is only eight miles long and can be knocked off in a day if you really know what you're doing. And if you really, really know what

THE CUILLIN RIDGE

N

0 ———— 1 mile

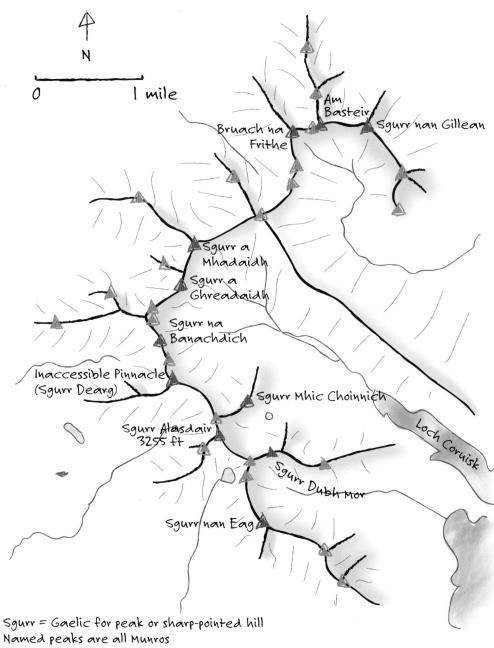

Am Basteir

Sgurr nan Gillean

Bruach na Frithe

Sgurr a Mhadaidh

Sgurr a Ghreadaidh

Sgurr na Banachdich

Inaccessible Pinnacle (Sgurr Dearg)

Sgurr Mhic Choinnich

Sgurr Alasdair 3255 ft

Loch Coruisk

Sgurr Dubh Mor

Sgurr nan Eag

Sgurr = Gaelic for peak or sharp-pointed hill
Named peaks are all Munros
i.e. mountains in Scotland above
3,000 ft. There are 11 Munros on the main Cuillin Ridge
out of 282 in Scotland. Some hikers spend half
a life time 'bagging', as it's known, all the Munros.

you're doing, you can complete it in two hours, 59 minutes and 22 seconds. That's how long it took Finlay Wild in 2013 when he set a new record for running the ridge.

But the numbers don't tell the whole story. While other ridge walks may be longer, or higher, this challenge takes its toll on even the best climbers. Island guides estimate that only one in ten people successfully complete the Summer Traverse.

MALEVOLENT MOUNTAINS

What makes it so testing? There's the sudden changes in elevation for a start – more than 12,000 ft of ascents and descents. Then there's the notoriously unpredictable Scottish weather; blue skies and sunshine one minute, gales and Arctic wind-chill the next – and that's just in summer. Much of the ridge is right on Skye's sea coast. This makes for some picture-perfect scenery but means there's absolutely nothing to shield you from the weather coming in from the water.

Even the mountains themselves seem out to get you. The Cuillin stone contains magnetic properties which can make a mess of navigation equipment (see sidebar); the basalt rock near the summit can be as slippery as ice when wet and many of the slopes are covered in scree – loose shards of rock which are a nightmare to negotiate.

To conquer the ridge, it's not enough to be a good technical climber, you have to be at the top of your game as a scrambler and navigator, too. No wonder it messes with so many people's heads.

For most people the Summer Traverse of the Cuillin Ridge is a two-day challenge and it deserves proper preparation. You'll need to

be confident at working a rope and physically capable of handling two days of constant climbing, scrambling and descending on difficult surfaces. You'll also need to work without a rope on some of the scrambling sections, an experience which some climbers can find unnerving. You'll probably have to bivouac overnight on the ridge, which brings its own

HARD ROCK & HEAVY METAL

Many rock formations include metallic deposits which can disrupt navigation equipment. The Cuillin Range is notorious for it – so forget about relying on a compass to find your way. Instead you'll need a proper GPS navigation device which you can use to take map readings. Don't even think about taking on the ridge without proper navigation kit and speak to local guides and climbers for their advice well in advance of your trip. The weather can change without a moment's notice; rain, hail, mist and snow can hit suddenly at any time of year and on some sections there is no margin for error. A wrong turn means a long drop.

logistical challenges, but also means you'll be nodding off and waking up to some of the finest vistas on planet Earth. You'll look down on one side at a seascape, dotted with islands big and small, and up at the spectacular ridge ahead of you on the other. There are worse ways to start a day.

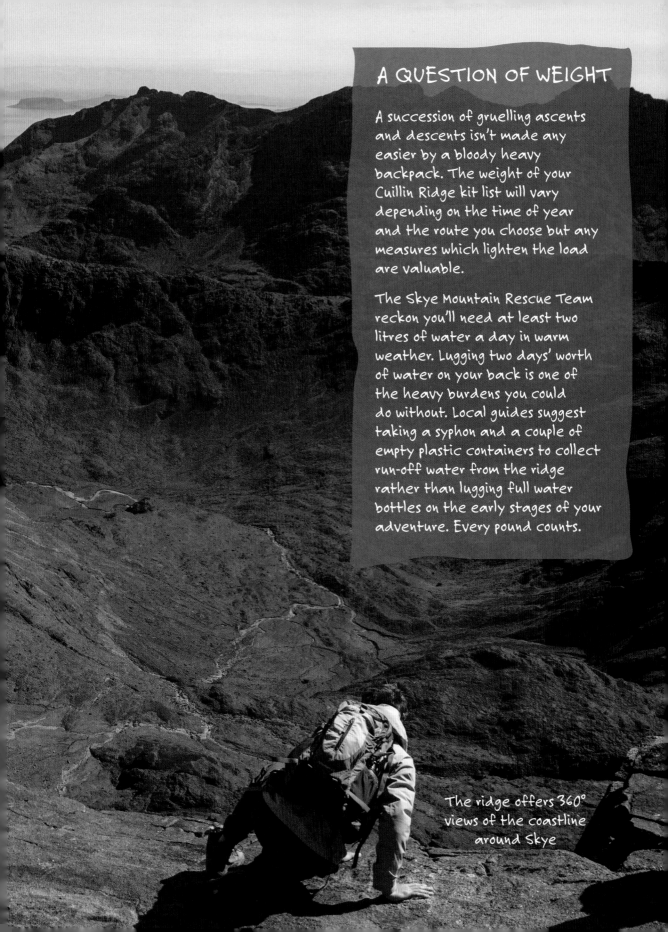

A QUESTION OF WEIGHT

A succession of gruelling ascents and descents isn't made any easier by a bloody heavy backpack. The weight of your Cuillin Ridge kit list will vary depending on the time of year and the route you choose but any measures which lighten the load are valuable.

The Skye Mountain Rescue Team reckon you'll need at least two litres of water a day in warm weather. Lugging two days' worth of water on your back is one of the heavy burdens you could do without. Local guides suggest taking a syphon and a couple of empty plastic containers to collect run-off water from the ridge rather than lugging full water bottles on the early stages of your adventure. Every pound counts.

The ridge offers 360° views of the coastline around Skye

Most local guides advise giving yourself a few days to explore the area, test the ground and get a feel for the exposed conditions. Unlike many other ridge walks, there's no dawdling through the foothills or long-distance hike to reach the start point. Once you've done the prep and checked the forecasts for a decent window of weather, you get straight into it.

THE 'IN PINN'

Tackling the ridge from south to north, the real fun kicks off at the 'In Pinn' – short for Inaccessible Pinnacle. It's an enormous slab of rock which juts 150 ft up from the ridge, as if the mountain is giving God the middle finger. The climb up and

abseil down will get your heart pumping and, if anything, the challenge gets more intense after that. There's a series of really technical climbs and descents, interspersed with tough scrambles along narrow scree-covered ridges. There's just no let-up until bedtime.

Day two is more of the same. A precise technical ascent here, a brutal energy sapping scramble there. Finally, with your fingers bleeding, your quads burning and your lungs bursting, you reach the fearsome Basteir Tooth. For many this jagged basalt column (remember basalt, the stone that becomes treacherously slippery when wet) is a climb too far. To have come so far and come up short is a brutal blow but this tooth bites and demands respect.

The Cuillin Ridge

And then... it's over. The descent is long and gentle. You follow a path down a beautiful glen and end up at an inn at the bottom which serves good beer and has hot showers.

Nowhere is quite like the Cuillin Ridge. It takes a certain kind of mental strength to process the varied challenges you'll face. If you've done it once, you'll want to try it again and explore more. You could head to Zion National Park in Utah, USA, where the ascent of Lady Mountain is one of the finest day-long scrambles you can find, or head to the High Atlas range in Morocco, to plot a route through some of Africa's toughest mountain terrain.

OTHER RIDGE WALKS

THE HIGH ATLAS RANGE, MOROCCO

Take in a beguiling mix of ancient terraced villages, hidden passes and towering peaks on North Africa's highest mountain range. The dry air at high altitude is both invigorating and demanding as you explore a succession of ridges which look like sharp folds in the landscape. The High Atlas range runs for some 450 miles and exploring the lot will take you years. Try a guided loop of the area round Toubkal, which at 13,167-feet is North Africa's highest mountain. In addition to the summit route itself, there are thrilling scrambles such as the section between the summits of Aksoual (12,835-feet) and Tamadoute (12,605-feet). Further east, the Mgoun Ridge flirts with mile after mile of thousand-foot drops.

KOPRA RIDGE, NEPAL

Many visitors to Nepal strike out for Everest base camp or the Annapurna Circuit but the smart travellers make for this little slice of Himalayan heaven which skirts the world's deepest gorge.

You'll get incredible views of Annapurna South, Annapurna 1 and Dhaulagiri (the seventh-highest mountain in the world) and will bed down in tiny villages where most of the accommodation is community-owned, meaning you're helping to sustain the way of life for future generations.

ZION NATIONAL PARK, UTAH, USA

Jam-packed with short-sweet ridge scrambles. Day-long trails like Lady Mountain and Angel's Landing lead you to spectacular viewpoints of a flame-red desert landscape.

HELL OR WHITE WATER

River rafting

Everyone tucks down, their sodden fingers scrabbling for the handles. Just in time - with a stomach-flipping lurch the raft plunges into a hole of swirling water, accelerating as it drops. Immediately the savage river rolls over a submerged boulder, forcing the raft skyward and compressing your spine with the instant acceleration. For a single heartbeat, the raft hangs in the air, almost vertical - a surreal, frozen moment.

But gravity always wins and the back of the raft slams into a huge boulder, flipping the whole world upside down. The shock of the cold water hits you like a sledgehammer. You gasp for a breath in a small pocket of air under the boat.

Now the current has your body in its jaws, dragging you downstream, utterly powerless. Another rapid and your legs thump against the river bed. You're in a spot of bother here.

Lungs burning, you kick up and resurface to the roar of the white water. Paddles and fellow rafters whirl around you like toys. Hacking, you cough up half the river.

Then - suddenly - all is calm.

Some of your companions have reached the shoreline. They flop onto a sandbar like drowned rats. Only a dozen or so rapids to go... bring them on!

THE MIGHTY ZAMBEZI
The river that thunders

Grade 5 rapid classification
Very powerful rapids with very confused and broken water, large drops, violent and fast currents, abrupt turns, difficult powerful stoppers and fast boiling eddies; with numerous obstacles in the main current. Complex, precise and powerful sequential manoeuvring is required. A definite risk to personal safety exists.

WITH A GUIDE
DIFFICULTY *******
ENDURANCE *******
NERVES OF STEEL ********

DURATION: FROM A DAY TO A WEEK
PERSONNEL: HALF A DOZEN PLUS GUIDE
SKILLSET: GOOD LEVEL OF GENERAL FITNESS, CONFIDENT SWIMMER
RISKS: HEAD INJURIES, DROWNING, CROCS!

SOUTHERN AFRICA

Turn up, pay your money, get in a raft, off you go. Doesn't sound too hardcore does it? Why not just pitch up at the bottom of Victoria Falls with your buddies, inflate your boat and take to the water? Because if you do that, chances are you'll all be dead within half an hour, that's why.

The only way to ride the rapids of the insanely powerful Zambezi river is on a commercial rafting trip. But this is a trip like no other and there aren't enough superlatives to do it justice.

Even many white-water professionals have said it would terrify them to have a boat full of customers on this river. If it were all guides they'd still be a little nervous.

For starters, before you get in the boat you need to do a pretty difficult climb down to the river. This steep route demands fitness and a head for heights. This ain't no cosy theme park ride.

It has taken the Zambezi millions of years to carve an 800-ft gouge into the rock. And if it can

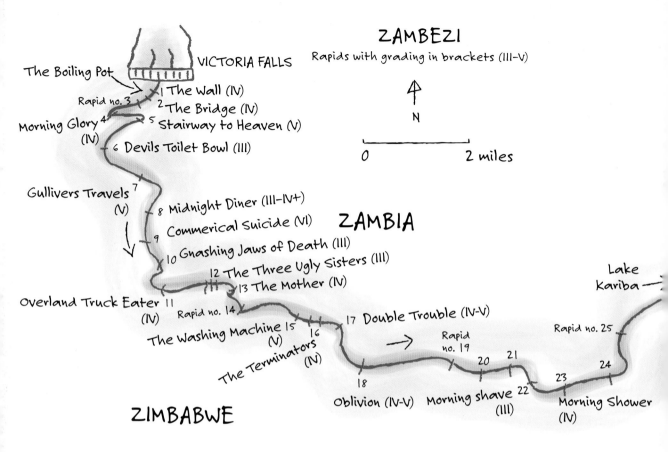

ZAMBEZI

Rapids with grading in brackets (III-V)

N

0 —— 2 miles

VICTORIA FALLS

The Boiling Pot

1 The Wall (IV)

Rapid no. 3

2 The Bridge (IV)

5 Stairway to Heaven (V)

Morning Glory 4 (IV)

6 Devils Toilet Bowl (III)

Gullivers Travels 7 (V)

8 Midnight Diner (III-IV+)

ZAMBIA

9 Commerical Suicide (VI)

10 Gnashing Jaws of Death (III)

12 The Three Ugly Sisters (III)

13 The Mother (IV)

Overland Truck Eater 11 (IV)

Rapid no. 14

17 Double Trouble (IV-V)

Lake Kariba →

The Washing Machine 15 (V)

16 The Terminators (IV)

Rapid no. 19

Rapid no. 25

20 21

24

18

23

ZIMBABWE

Oblivion (IV-V)

Morning shave 22 (III)

Morning Shower (IV)

---

carve hard basalt, it can carve you. At the height of the wet season, 20 million cubic feet of water per minute tumble over the Victoria Falls, then through the narrow gorges below. Unsurprisingly, the river is off-limits to commercial rafting until water levels calm down.

GNASHING JAWS OF DEATH

Devil's Toilet Bowl; The Washing Machine; Overland Truck Eater; Gnashing Jaws of Death. These are some of the charming nicknames of the more testing rapids. See for yourself whether you think they merit them. Certainly the pro rafters believe they do – no other commercially rafted river in the world has such a high concen-

tration of Grade 4 and 5 rapids. Depending on water levels it's necessary to bypass some when they are too deadly to ride. Rapid no. 9, the quaintly named 'Commercial Suicide', is classed as a Grade 6 and always avoided. As you hike around it you might see a crazy kayaker trying their luck and be glad you're on dry land.

Some people who sign up for a day trip bail out at lunchtime, traumatized by the whole experience. Fortunately, the professional guides on the Zambezi are among the best in the business. If you're nervous, seek out the guides with the most experience, many of whom see a boat flip as a professional embarrassment. This section of the Zambezi is a pool-drop river which means there isn't too much exposed rock in the

Nile crocs won't bother you... probably

rapids or in the pools below. The day trip covers 15 miles, over which the river drops 400 ft.

To escape from the crowds (or if one day of insane adrenaline isn't enough) you can take several days to travel the full 75 miles through the gorge, camping en route, all the way to Lake Kariba. Most of the big rapids are behind you once the day trippers are done but this mighty river has a few stings in its tail. These include the Chamamba and Upper Moemba rapids and the pièce de résistance and big finale – 'Ghostrider' – the wildest and longest of all of the rapids on the Zambezi. It just seems to go on and on forever. Unfortunately, once the Batoka Gorge dam (see sidebar) is built, this classic rapid will disappear under a lake.

After this, there is more time to enjoy the scenery and the trip turns into a safari after the white-knuckle ride. On the river banks you'll see, and hear, Chacma baboons, and in the river, often worryingly close, 12-ft long Nile crocodiles and hippos. All this, plus glorious African sunsets – what more could you ask for?

Finally, remember that there is one very good thing about getting flung out of your raft and swirled around like you're in a giant washing machine: it cleans the seat of your pants beautifully.

A DAM CONTROVERSY

If you fancy a rafting trip here you'd best be quick because there are plans to construct a huge dam further downstream at the Batoka Gorge. This will submerge some of the best rapids – what a pity. It's not clear how many will be lost and it's possible the resulting reservoir will flood the river to within half a mile of Victoria Falls. The battle to save the river is far from over but it would be a tragedy if this rafting trip was consigned to history.

RIVER RAPID CLASSIFICATION

Rapids are classified on a scale of 1–6. Grade 1 being a bit bumpy and Grade 6 classed as 'life-threatening'. As there is not much money in tourists dying by the boatload, Grade 6 rapids are not rafted commercially. These are for the elite, requiring careful inspection, and when water conditions are favourable. Mistakes made during descent will have dire consequences.

The grade of a rapid can vary depending on fluctuating water levels. Usually higher water levels will make the rapid more difficult. However, when water levels are low, more obstacles in the river may become exposed, increasing the risk of head injury should rafters end up in the water.

You might get wet!

THE COLORODO, A JOURNEY FROM HISTORY

The Colorado River is 1,450 miles long, rising two miles high in the Rockies and draining parts of seven US and two Mexican states on its way to the Gulf of California. It is a natural barrier par excellence. Sheer cliffs on both sides run for hundreds of miles, boxing you into a series of deep canyons – the real world can feel a long way above your head. One of these gorges is the fabled Grand Canyon, a mile-deep scar in the Earth cut by the river over millions of years. Add in wild meanders, deadly rapids, waterfalls and whirlpools and you have 1,450 miles of rafting heaven.

The Colorado offers some of the biggest and most challenging white water in North America. For many, a multi-day rafting trip down the Colorado, camping out in remote canyons along the way, is the adventure of a lifetime. The scenery is awe-inspiring but it comes with a unique twist – you are following the route of one of the world's all-time great explorations.

In 1869 nobody had ventured down this river. No one even knew what was at the bottom of the gorge. As well as the sheer physical danger of the canyon, there was also something of a hoodoo about the place. The native Americans believed the gods had made it impassable and anyone who tried to enter the mighty canyons would perish.

To John Wesley Powell, however, this all made it simply irresistible. Risking drowning, starvation, heat exhaustion and deadly attacks by native Americans, Powell's expedition was the first scientific exploration of large stretches of the Green and Colorado Rivers and the first to map one of the wildest rivers on the planet.

The Colorado in the
Grand Canyon

DISASTER FALLS

Powell's expedition was only two weeks old and negotiating a tributary of the Colorado when disaster struck for the first of many times. The wooden boats were cruising through a peaceful canyon when Powell noticed white water ahead. He pulled in to the shore and ordered the other pilots to follow, but the crew of a following boat missed his warning and floated on past. By the time they heard his frantic shouts it was too late — the current took hold and pulled them down a series of crashing rapids.

The three crew were thrown overboard into the maelstrom and their boat was smashed into pieces against a fist of boulders. Horror-struck, Powell and the others scrabbled over the rocks to save their stricken crewmates. The three men

were nowhere to be seen at first. Then, one by one, the bedraggled survivors hauled themselves on to the rocky riverbank. They had narrowly escaped drowning but many of the party's clothes, guns, personal possessions and a large amount of food were gone. Powell named the rapids Disaster Falls and the island that the boat washed up on Disaster Island.

This rapid typified what lay ahead for Powell and his men. One member of the party bailed a few weeks later after proclaiming that he had "seen danger enough". Three more departed further down-river but were killed by hostile native American tribespeople. Of the 10 expedition members that started out from Green River Station, only six completed the three-month journey to claim their place in history.

RUNNING THE RAPIDS

The beauty of guided white-water rafting is that even if you're a novice you can dive into nature at its rawest. The options below are extreme, but many rivers, just a few miles from the bustle of a city, can provide a wilderness experience that can cleanse the soul. Mindfulness is about paying attention to the here and now. When you are rafting a wild river, your brain switches off from everything else. The only thought in your head is making it through the next rapid.

SUN KOSI RIVER, NEPAL

This seven-to-nine-day trip through the foothills of the Himalayas is the longest in Nepal and arguably the best central Asia has to offer. Along the 170-mile trip down the Sun Kosi River to its confluence with the Ganges, you'll journey through dense tropical jungle, narrow gorges, forested canyons and several Grade 5 rapids. Peg out your tent on white sandy river beaches, offer thanks at remote Hindu temples and shower in some of the beautiful waterfalls you'll pass along the way.

NORTH JOHNSTONE RIVER, NORTHERN QUEENSLAND, AUSTRALIA

You're helicoptered into the middle of the rainforest to reach the start point – how cool is that? On the voyage through thick woods, you'll pass trees that were sprouting when Nero was fiddling in Rome. If you're lucky (or unlucky depending on your point of view), you'll see saltwater crocs, pythons and bird spiders. When darkness falls, read your book by the light of the luminous fungi on the canyon walls. Oh, and the Grade 4 and 5 rapids are quite interesting.

KAITUNA RIVER, NEW ZEALAND

The highlight of this Grade 5 river near Rotorua is the 23-feet-high Tutea Falls. It's the highest commercially rafted waterfall in the world.

"Setting yourself a challenge to survive in the wilderness might sound like a geeky thing to do. Actually, it can give you a sense of confidence knowing that you can look after yourself and your family should the unexpected happen."

DESERT ISLAND RISKS

Island survival

Gentle waves lap against your feet as you watch a vivid orange sun slowly sink down to embrace the distant horizon. There's not a cloud in the sky and a gentle breeze softly caresses your skin as you sink back onto powdery sand and allow yourself a small, satisfied grin. This is the life. A tropical paradise all to yourself. No ringing phones, no status updates, no crowded commutes to a joyless office. Just you, the beach, the sea and day after day of fun in the sun.

What a load of rubbish.

Being marooned on a desert island is not the romantic experience that you are expecting. For a start, it's hard work in the blistering sun just to do the basic things that keep you alive. It's hard to enjoy a sunset when you don't have water. It's hard to see the beauty in a fish when you haven't eaten in days. You long to relax but there is so much to do. And if you are alone the intensity of the pressure to perform is unexplainable. The only way to know what it's like is to feel it for yourself.

VAVA'U ISLANDS, TONGA

Set yourself one of the most primitive survival challenges of all – finding a way to live on an uninhabited island. You'll face the constant physical and mental pressure of getting the basic resources humans need to subsist.

DIFFICULTY *****

ENDURANCE *****

NERVES OF STEEL ***✴✴

DURATION: 14 DAYS OR MORE

PERSONNEL: JUST YOU, OBVIOUSLY

SKILLSET: FIREMAKING, HUNTING, FISHING, FORAGING, MENTAL FORTITUDE

RISKS: STARVATION, ILLNESS, MENTAL DISINTEGRATION

VANUATU

SAMOA

HA'APAI GROUP

NEW CALEDONIA

FIJI

VAVA'U GROUP

TONGA

South Pacific Ocean

TONGATAPU GROUP

COOK ISLANDS

NEW ZEALAND

The Kingdom of Tonga is a group of 169 small islands spread out over an area of the South Pacific the size of Texas. Only 36 of those islands are inhabited, which gives you a pretty decent selection of empty islands to choose from. Many of these are handily placed – just over the horizon from a populated centre – which means you'll be isolated but rescuable. If you have decided to go through with the full-on challenge of marooning yourself the Vava'u group, in the Kingdom's northern reaches, is the place for you.

There are more than 60 islands and atolls here. Some are sand-fringed, encircled by coral reefs; some burst out of the ocean with dramatic coastal cliffs and cave systems. Many of them, crucially, are human-free. The region's climate is another attraction. Avoid the cyclone season, which runs from April to November, and the dry winter months of July and August. And, for heaven's sake, choose an island with a clean source of drinking water – relying on rain for your water supply is like playing a game of Russian roulette with the weather gods.

THE INNER BATTLE

If spending an extended length of time alone on an uninhabited island is such a dangerous ordeal, why try and do it? It's a fair question. Foraging for food is an ongoing challenge and one that you can't afford to lose. You can cope without sustenance for, say, four to five days. Any longer than that and it's frightening how

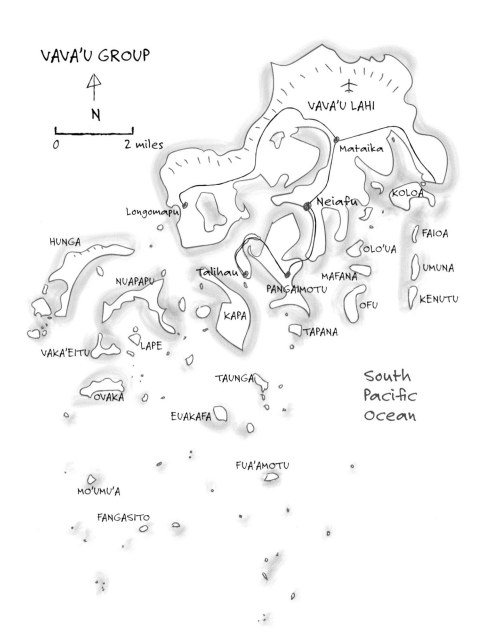

VAVA'U GROUP

N

0   2 miles

VAVA'U LAHI

Mataika

KOLOA

Longomapu

Neiafu

FAIOA

OLO'UA

HUNGA

UMUNA

Talihau

MAFANA

NUAPAPU

KENUTU

PANGAIMOTU

KAPA

OFU

LAPE

TAPANA

VAKA'EITU

South
Pacific
Ocean

TAUNGA

OVAKA

EUAKAFA

FUA'AMOTU

MO'UMU'A

FANGASITO

quickly your body caves in on itself. Add in the mental pressure that comes with total isolation and the dangers are all too real.

Those are the risks. So what are the rewards? If the threats to your wellbeing are pretty basic, then so are the benefits. It's essentially a system reboot for your soul. When you are alone with only the contents of your own brain for company, there's no hiding place from the thoughts and emotions that are so easy to shove into the background during the course of everyday, normal, not-marooned-on-a-desert-island, life.

Securing the things you take so readily for granted in civilian life will give you the most intense highs in these constrained circumstances. You'll be giddy with excitement when a sudden rain shower fills your makeshift liquid containers, giggling like a kid at Christmas as you glug down the most beautiful water you've ever tasted. You'll feel profoundly satisfied knowing that the massive lump of dead wood you've spent all day hauling across the island will keep you warm and cook your meals for at least a couple of days.

THE STONE CIRCLE

In the modern world we are rarely truly alone, especially for lengthy periods. Even when we are, we have a whole manner of distractions. It may be as simple as picking up the phone and chatting to someone that lifts our mood.

On a desert island there is no one to bounce ideas off. You are truly alone and isolated from everything and everyone you have ever known. You might be on dry land but this feeling of isolation is like floating in space, or swimming in the deepest parts of the farthest ocean. This sense of limitlessness can cause you to panic.

So, how do you cope?

One suggestion is to create a pseudo physical boundary to help make sense of it all. Just about anything can be used to construct this safe zone. For some people it might be a square

carved in sand on the beach or the confines of a tree's bough.

For one bewildered, terrified castaway on an island in Fiji, it was a circle of stones. Before reaching the island, an Aboriginal Australian friend suggested sitting inside this circle when things became difficult. He promised that, within the circle, the spirit of his ancestors would provide a safe haven from the isolation-induced terrors that would surely lie ahead.

And, know what? It worked. The power of believing in the circle's protection was enough to provide comfort and courage. Each island survivor's method of finding a safe place will be different. It won't necessarily be a systematic collection of rocks. But on a desert island, everyone needs some kind of stone circle.

Vava'u islands

ISLAND LIFE HACKS

MUD... makes a pretty good... sunblock.
A decent coating of mud will shield you from the most harmful effects of the sun. You won't look a million dollars but nobody is going to notice, are they?

CHARCOAL... makes a pretty good... toothpaste.
A bit of charcoal on your finger is all you need to keep your teeth nice and clean. Don't do it too often, though, or the first thing you'll need when you get back to civilization is a trip to the dentists.

POO... makes a pretty good... fish bait.
Human eats fish. Human poops fish remains. Fish eats poo. Human catches fish eating poo. It's a circle of life thing. Just make sure you give your supper a really good wash first.

COCONUT OIL... makes a pretty good... skin cream.
Leave coconut flesh in the sun and collect the oil as it seeps out. It makes a pretty good balm for chafing from saltwater.

In a short time, these moments, during which your brain allows you to feel safe and secure, will make your heart soar more than any of the most luxurious trappings of modern life. But even while your brain is congratulating you for meeting its most primeval urges, it's also taunting you with the prospect that these good times won't last. It's at times like this you realize what's really important, and what really isn't. In other circumstances that might just be a cliché. On your island, it's the truth. And that's why you're there.

STRESSFUL TIMES

As the days pass, you'll be incredibly busy with the physical business of surviving, but it becomes impossible not to start dipping into some serious soul searching. It happens because you feel vulnerable in your own company and there is no way of diluting the doubts and fears you will inevitably have. There are no distractions or diversions. There is nowhere to hide and that can be bloody terrifying.

You'll need to find some way of processing your thoughts and feelings if you want to get off the island again in one psychological piece. Managing the stress of island isolation will be your biggest test – but only just. The vexingly difficult trial of keeping yourself fed, watered and sheltered is a very close second.

Mention a desert island expedition to some people and they respond with all sorts of nonsense about living off nature's bounty; supping coconut milk in a shack built from driftwood with a nice, juicy fish roasting over a roaring fire, probably with a volleyball called Wilson to keep you company.

The reality is so much less glamorous and more exhausting. Take drinking water, the absolute fundamental requirement for any survival mission. Finding a source of fresh water can be devilishly difficult and relying on liquid from coconuts is going to mess about with your bowels in a really explosive way. So you adapt, you evolve, you make the most of any opportunity that presents itself. Any source of clean water is to be cherished; any rainfall

"Eat what you can, when you can"

a chance to stock up your reservoirs. Foraging for food is a constant challenge, too, but manageable so long as you're not a fussy eater. After all, a bit of raw fish never hurt anyone. Well, almost anyone.

HUNTING & GATHERING

The most physically demanding requirement will be the hunt for firewood. The ability to start a blaze and keep it going is vital for all sorts of reasons; for warmth at night, for cooking food and for morale – the feeling of knowing you are mastering your domain. Within a few days, it's more than likely you'll have exhausted all the firewood within the immediate area of your camp. You'll have to travel further for your supplies as time goes by and spend more time and energy lugging it all back to camp. Surprisingly, perhaps, wood gathering feels pretty rewarding. It feels as if you're doing what needs to be done; as if you're coping.

Once you've managed to find a way of providing the essentials you need to survive, the nature of your solitary adventure will start to change. You'll become more aware of your surroundings. You'll notice details on the landscape that your mind did not compute when it was in survival mode, like differences in the species of trees and the distinctive calls of island birdlife.

At this point you've found a way to survive. The question becomes, how long do you want to live like this? There is no right or wrong answer. For some people this might be just a few days, for others, much, much longer. The length of time is less important than what you learn while you're there. It's not about your body, or your mind. It's about your soul and living instinctively. The self-discoveries you make here will change your life.

ISLAND LIFE

ÅLAND ISLANDS, FINLAND

This archipelago in the Baltic Sea consists of more than 6,500 islands, only 35 of which are inhabited. There's plenty of scope to head out by boat from Mariehamn, the islands' only town, and be in splendid isolation within a few hours. Timing your trip will have a big impact on the nature of your challenge. Temperatures hover around freezing in the winter months, and can plunge much lower on occasion. High summer is full of long days and heavy rain showers. It's also the time of year when you're most likely to encounter some adventurous day trippers landing on your island, which might somewhat ruin the mood. Aim for the shoulder seasons of April/May and September/October, when it never gets properly warm or terribly cold. Most islands have a smattering of tree cover and the Baltic here is rich with marine life, which makes Åland a decent shout for an introduction to island survival.

ORINOCO ISLANDS, VENEZUELA

Uninhabited islands aren't only found in the open seas. The mighty Orinoco, which flows more than 1,300 miles north through Venezuela, has dozens of them. The delta, where the river empties into the Atlantic Ocean, is a massive jigsaw of forest-coated islands that see no human activity. Up river, deep in the equatorial rainforest, are fluvial islands measuring up to a mile long where a combination of fast-flowing water and thick vegetation acts as an isolating barrier every bit as effective as hundreds of miles of sea.

TETEPARE, SOLOMON ISLANDS

The South Pacific's largest uninhabited island is not technically deserted but it's close enough to meet your needs. A small ecolodge, run by descendants of the people who last lived on the island around one hundred years ago, services

The Åland Islands.
Well, some of them.

tourists at certain times of year. If you can negotiate access to the island when there are no parties at the lodge, you'll have 46 square miles of hills, trees, beaches and reefs all to yourself.

MALDIVES, INDIAN OCEAN

A great place to explore if you don't have an appetite for complete desertion. Many tours and resorts offer the chance to experience seclusion on one of the 900-odd uninhabited land masses that pepper the ocean - with the added convenience of only having to survive for a day or two.

THE OPEN ROAD

Driving challenges

Hardcore travellers may have some reservations about going on a long-distance road trip. Automotive travel cuts you off from your surroundings, the argument goes, and dulls the feeling of travelling in different cultures and landscapes. Perhaps there's some truth to that. Some people drive from point to point on a map with barely a stop, trying to cram in as many miles as possible and tick off as many destinations before they fly home.

It doesn't have to be that way. A road trip can be a hugely rewarding, immersive experience. The key is to recognize that travelling in your vehicle is a means to an end, not the end itself.

The big advantage of having a vehicle is that you can create your own schedule. This means you can rip it up and make a new one if you find an interesting detour that requires exploration. If you stumble upon a great spot, you have the freedom to make camp for as long as you like.

A 'real' road trip is a gift to yourself. So strap yourself in, aim at a horizon and open your mind to the drive of a lifetime.

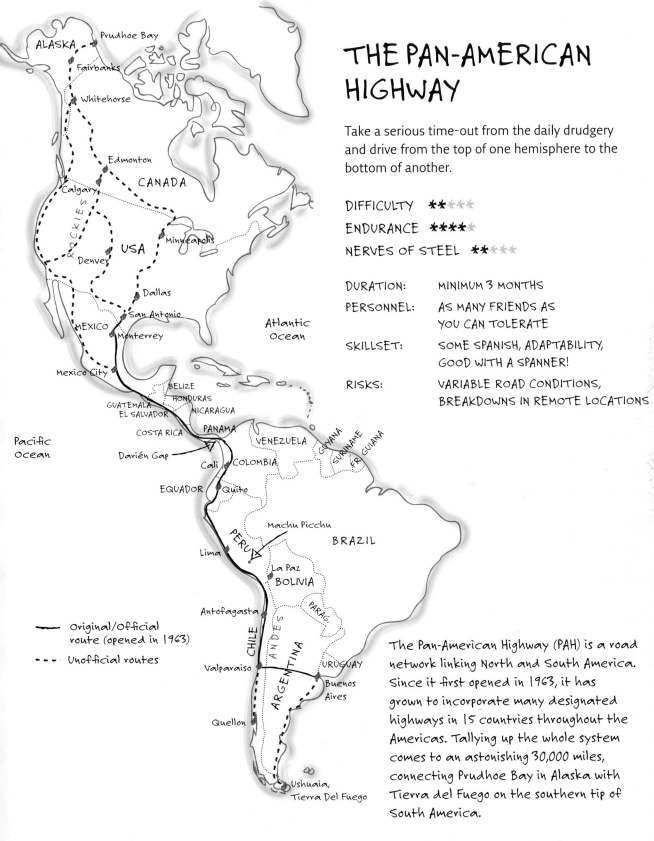

THE PAN-AMERICAN HIGHWAY

Take a serious time-out from the daily drudgery and drive from the top of one hemisphere to the bottom of another.

DIFFICULTY ★★☆☆☆

ENDURANCE ★★★★☆

NERVES OF STEEL ★★☆☆☆

DURATION: MINIMUM 3 MONTHS

PERSONNEL: AS MANY FRIENDS AS YOU CAN TOLERATE

SKILLSET: SOME SPANISH, ADAPTABILITY, GOOD WITH A SPANNER!

RISKS: VARIABLE ROAD CONDITIONS, BREAKDOWNS IN REMOTE LOCATIONS

— Original/Official route (opened in 1963)

- - - Unofficial routes

The Pan-American Highway (PAH) is a road network linking North and South America. Since it first opened in 1963, it has grown to incorporate many designated highways in 15 countries throughout the Americas. Tallying up the whole system comes to an astonishing 30,000 miles, connecting Prudhoe Bay in Alaska with Tierra del Fuego on the southern tip of South America.

Pan-American Highway,
Nazca Plateau, Peru

Most long-distance road trips involving multiple countries require fairly extensive planning. Making progress through Africa or Asia can be a sticky, morale-sapping mess of red tape and travel guidance updates which can take months to sort and really knock the wind out of your sails.

For those with jobs, mortgages and all the other trappings of a busy life, if the planning stage takes too long, the doubts can creep in and you're in danger of talking yourself out of the whole thing.

This is where the Pan-American Highway plays its ace card. If you're based in North America, or can get there pretty easily, with the exception of a couple of vaccinations, you can literally just get to the start and make the rest up as you go along. You don't even need to take a car – you can just buy a vehicle at your starting point and then flog it where you finish. Language considerations are not insurmountable either. If you have a basic grasp of Spanish, or are willing to learn en route, you'll do just fine.

THE OFFICIAL ROUTE

Starting at Laredo in Mexico, just over the border from San Antonio, Texas, the original – and still official – route goes all the way to Buenos Aires in Argentina.

On the way south, the PAH goes through every ecological and climatic zone, from snowy mountain passes to dense tropical jungle and deserts. The straight-line distance is 18,000 miles but there is a section which is tarmac-free for some 62 miles, right in the middle – the notorious Darién Gap in Panama and Colombia. There's a very good reason for this missing link in the chain (see panel on page 130). To continue your journey, it's necessary to ship your vehicle between ports and make your way through on public transport.

In Central America, the PAH goes through all the capital cities with the exception of Honduras. Sorry, Tegucigalpa, it's nothing personal. In Mexico there is a separate branch to give you the option of following the coastline on the Pacific side of the country before rejoining the main route. After Belize, Honduras and El Salvador, Nicaragua awaits you. A worthy side trip is to swing by Lake Nicaragua, climb aboard a ferry and explore a few of the lake's 300 islands. Be careful if you dip your toes in the water, though. This freshwater lake is patrolled by man-eating bull sharks.

Once past the Darién Gap the PAH follows the western side of South America, first through Colombia and then Ecuador's welcoming capital, Quito. The opportunities to stop are almost infinite but if you can only pick one country to spend an extended period in, put Ecuador at the top of your list.

Why Ecuador? For starters, you can hike the three-to-four-day Quilotoa Loop around its spectacular crater lake in the Ecuadorian Andes. Or go on a week-long jungle tour in

FASTEST & SLOWEST

* American Tim Cahill and Canadian Garry Sowerby drove north from Ushuaia to Prudhoe Bay in less than 24 days. They probably didn't do much in the way of sightseeing.

* British adventurer George Meegan did the route on foot in the early 1980s, taking 2,425 days to walk between Tierra del Fuego and Alaska.

Yasuní National Park to see Ecuador's incredible wildlife – a terrific and cheaper alternative to the Galápagos Islands. The town of Tena is a great base for exploring Ecuador's Amazon jungle and also offers great opportunities for white-water rafting and kayaking. Oh, and don't forget Quito itself. Surrounded by Andean peaks, walk the cobbled streets of this beautiful colonial city until your feet can take no more.

The PAH then takes you through Peru for 1,500 miles before entering northern Chile. Here you're presented with another big fork in the road. There's an option to continue down the western flank of the Andes, or you can stick to the main route and head east towards Buenos Aires. Another branch will take you to Rio de Janeiro

or you can keep heading south towards Tierra del Fuego. The scenery on this final southern stretch, as you head towards the end of the road, is mesmerizingly beautiful.

LIFE ON THE ROAD

That's the directions taken care of. But what's it really like to travel? It very much depends why you want to do it. If your intention is to drive it in the shortest possible time to boast that you did it in one month with just a few selfie stops as you go, then really, what is the point? You'll likely learn nothing about the places you visit or about yourself because the real adventure begins when you take detours, stop for a few weeks or longer,

TOP TIPS

* Cashing in your car: Argentina and Chile have laws preventing the immediate sale of imported vehicles so check the rules. Cars can be sold in the Chilean free-trade zones of Puerto Arenas in the south and Iquique in the north.

* Border business: Make your crossing early in the morning to avoid queues. Most crossings close at night and aren't pleasant places to hang about after dark so plan ahead.

* Friendly firefighters: Having car trouble? Can't get to a garage? Many PAH veterans suggest your next best hope for help may be a local fire station.

* Take your time: However you choose to tackle the PAH, the one thing you'll need in abundance is patience. Make sure you're in sync with the priorities of the people and places you're visiting.

* Get clear: Why opt for a 4x4 on your mammoth drive? It's got little to do with extra grip from four-wheeled propulsion and everything to do with extra ground clearance. Give your undercarriage air to avoid the worst potholes.

* If you choose to rely on Latin America's bus services, you'll get up close and personal with your fellow passengers. How many people can you get onto a Nicaraguan bus? Two more.

Quilotoa, Ecuador

Quito

THE DARIÉN GAP: THE LOST HIGHWAY

The PAH runs from the very top of the Americas to the very bottom. Well... almost. A short section in central America, where Panama and Columbia meet, isn't on the map. Did someone just forget about it? Nope – there are far more ominous reasons for this missing link. This section is the notorious Darién Gap. There are no roads, no bridges and no continuous tracks other than those used by the indigenous tribespeople of this lawless land. The Colombian side is swamp-ridden and the Panamanian side is spectacularly mountainous.

There are millions of square miles of impenetrable rainforest in a region frequented by drug traffickers. Add several objectionable mammal, reptile and insect species into the mix and you start to get an idea of how inhospitable a place it is. You might not be surprised to learn that the usual travel advice is to steer well clear.

Several attempts have been made to engineer a lasting route through this final section of the PAH but all have come to nothing. Perhaps it's no bad thing as the Darién Gap provides a useful barrier. It hinders the spread of diseases such as foot-and-mouth. Besides, there's something oddly comforting knowing there's a piece of the world that won't yield to motor vehicles.

Like an itch that just has to be scratched, though, various expeditions have attempted to conquer the Gap and drive the whole of the Americas. In 1972, a British expedition became the first to travel by vehicle from Alaska to Cape Horne. Led by Major John Blashford-Snell, the British Trans-Americas Expedition covered more than 18,000 miles in just over six months. Of those six months, it took three to negotiate 250 miles of roadless terrain through the Darién Gap. Blashford-Snell and his team coaxed two Range Rovers over rivers, through bogs and swamps for 96 murderous days – one of the greatest feats of vehicle-based exploration the world has ever seen.

The Darién Gap is a graveyard for even the toughest off-road vehicles

Quechua market traders, Bolivian Highlands

meet people and immerse yourself in the world that surrounds you. Perhaps you'll even give something back.

It took Ben Jamin from the island of Jersey three years to complete his journey on the Latin American section of the PAH, but not because he was a slow driver. His experiences encapsulate everything positive about this crazy road trip. Despite having no mechanical training or technical skills, he bought an old campervan in Chile, moved in with the family he bought it from for four months (though neither party spoke each other's language) and kitted out his camper before hitting the road.

On his journey north he offered a pick-up service for other travellers. Some stayed for a few hours; others tagged along for months and became lifelong friends in the process. However, more significantly, it was his immersion into

local life that made the trip special. In the Amazon he stayed with villagers unused to foreign visitors and went hunting with their children. In Costa Rica he stopped for three months and moved into a garage while he taught himself how to fix his engine. While the van was on bricks, he used his spare time to explore the country.

In El Salvador he offered free surfing trips; in Guatemala, after another engine blow-out, he stayed for five months in one village, becoming good friends with his neighbours. He even started an online fundraiser to help a villager suffering from cancer. And in the Belizean jungle, he worked for his keep on a family farm.

He had to fix or replace the engine *eleven* times over the three years. But, when you think about it, the engine woes were the making of Ben's odyssey. Most of his best stories and

Andes Salt Flats, Bolivia
(courtesy KombiLife)

Ushuaia,
Tierra del Fuego

memorable experiences took place when he was forced to stop, often for months at a time. Had the engine worked perfectly, he might have taken the same route but his journey would have been completely different and probably much less rewarding.

Not everyone has the luxury of having an infinite amount of time to do the trip. Nevertheless, there is a lesson to be learned. If the trip has to be completed within, say, four months, rather than stopping for a day here and a day there, why not get some miles in between stops and spend longer in just a handful of places?

Of course, there are some must-sees on the trip, such as the Inca Trail, Machu Picchu, Cuzco, the Panama Canal and the Patagonian Highlands, but to get the most from your trip, resist the temptation to turn it into a box-ticking exercise. That way, you can make up your own adventure and leave the crowds behind.

COST

How long is a piece of string? Ben took 1,000 days to complete the Latin American section of the PAH, spending an astonishingly frugal US $10-15 per day. He slept in his campervan, avoided tourist hotspots and ate where the locals ate. The hitchhikers he gave lifts to contributed to the fuel fund and he picked up odd jobs as and when cash was required.

More typically though, but still keeping luxuries to a minimum, spending around US $30,000 over two years, travelling solo in a 4x4, is realistic.

MORE GREAT ROAD TRIPS

CAIRO TO CAPE TOWN

The classic overland route through the heart of Africa is still a proper adventure – even if you do have air-conditioning and GPS these days.

You'll need six months minimum to do justice to the journey from Egypt's capital all the way to the Cape of Good Hope. The most popular route takes you down the continent's eastern seaboard into Sudan, Ethiopia, Kenya, Tanzania and Malawi. It then heads southwest through Zambia, Zimbabwe, Botswana, Namibia and finally South Africa.

It's a 6,500-mile drive if you follow the most direct route between Cairo and Cape Town, but this is no smoothly tarmacked autobahn. You'll drive on every possible road surface – many of which barely qualify as roads, to be honest. The only thing you can guarantee on this trip is that it definitely won't pan out the way you think it will.

Nevertheless, you should start with a detailed plan, even if it falls apart on day one. Some travel visas need to be organized before you go; others can be sorted while you're travelling. It's possible to go on guided self-drive holidays and these are still pretty full-on. For the real deal, organize it yourself but do your homework and be aware of the dangers. It is still the whole of Africa after all.

ICELAND'S RING ROAD

At 830 miles, Iceland's Ring Road can be done in just a week during the summer but that week packs a massive punch if you're into wild landscapes. Drive a couple of hours out from the capital, Reykjavik, and you'll feel like the last person on Earth – or some far-flung planet, more likely. You'll drive by glacial ice caves, volcanoes, geothermal springs, thundering waterfalls and, if you're lucky, witness

Iceland's ring road

the Northern Lights without any visual pollution from towns and cities.

Starting in Reykjavík, going clockwise, your first stopping point is the beautiful Hvalfjörður fjord. From there you can hike to the 650-foot-high Glymur waterfall. The next day you'll reach the amazing gorge at Kolugljúfur; push on to Akureyri and its terrific thermal pool for some relaxation. The main loop continues past volcanic craters, lava fields, glaciers and bubbling mud pots, each sight inviting you to max out the memory card in your camera. If you need a break from the scenery, Iceland's fascinating culture and wildlife will do the trick quite nicely.

To really get under the skin of Iceland, go for much longer than a week. Rent a four-wheel-drive vehicle, take a tent, plenty of food and water and leave the ring road.

INTO THE ABYSS
Dark water dives

You hover over the abyss, staring down past your fins into shades of blue that slowly melt into black. A diver above you disturbs some sand, which catches the sun and glitters briefly before it slowly disappears, into the depths.

In the near distance, a shark changes direction with a quick snap of its tail and glides towards you. A blacktip, a couple of yards long. You watch it swim by on your left at a range of about five feet.

No great danger there but these waters are also visited by hammerheads and bull sharks – an encounter with one of them could be a whole lot livelier.

You get the nod from your dive master and it's time to go. You look up into the brilliant, pale sky rippling above you, check your kit one more time, then begin your descent into darkness...

Miyakojima,
Okinawa, Japan

Lighthouse Reef and the Blue Hole

THE BLUE HOLE, BELIZE

A dark water dive awakens your soul. The lack of colour sharpens your other senses as you negotiate a part of our planet where humans barely dare to venture. It's a test of skill and nerve but, most of all, it's a form of release – trespassing in a foreign domain for a fleeting moment in time.

DIFFICULTY ***✩✩

ENDURANCE *✩✩✩✩

NERVES OF STEEL *****

DURATION: A DAY TO A WEEK

PERSONNEL: HALF A DOZEN PLUS GUIDE

SKILLSET: GOOD LEVEL OF GENERAL FITNESS, ADVANCED OPEN WATER DIVING

RISKS: HEAD INJURIES, DROWNING, CROCS!

Back in an age when Planet Earth was still young and frisky, the Blue Hole wasn't blue at all. It was above ground, a system of caverns in Central America, filled with nothing but fresh air and maybe a few bats. A succession of ice ages changed all that. Sea levels rose as the planet defrosted and the Hole was submerged beneath a blanket of water.

Fast forward a few millennia and this natural wonder, situated on a reef about 40 miles off the coast of Belize, is the location for an unforgetta-ble diving adventure. It's home to a fascinating array of marine life and boasts a stunning, ethereal, underwater landscape.

This natural wonder has become increasingly busy as the world's travel media trample over each other to give it more and more plaudits. In 2012 the Discovery Channel ranked the Blue Hole number one in its list of 'The World's Most Amazing Places'. Getting there is quite a slog. It's several hours in a small boat on choppy waters from the nearest landing point. Then there's the dive itself. It's very... well... *dark* down there. The bright and beautiful creatures you see zipping about the reefs at the surface are conspicuous by their absence. Finally, most Blue Hole dives don't tend to last very long – about 30 minutes is as much time as you'll get in most cases.

Why bother, you might ask? Put simply, there really isn't anywhere else like it on Earth. The Hole is the biggest submarine sinkhole in the world, measuring nearly 1,000 ft across and 400 ft deep. And, once you start exploring its depths, it enchants you in a way that's hard to explain with the rational parts of your brain.

GLOBAL FAME

The legendary French aquatic explorer Jacques Cousteau, who knew a thing or two about underwater marvels, visited the Blue Hole in the early 1970s and promptly declared it one of the best dive sites in the world. Since then, thousands more have agreed with Jacques.

It's not a dive for novices, though. To experience the Blue Hole in all its glory you'll need to commit to proper scuba training and be comfortable at diving to depths of up to 140 ft.

The dive itself begins sedately, with a drop of about 40 ft down to a sandy shelf which surrounds the Hole like an enormous basketball hoop. At this relatively shallow depth you'll be accompanied by all sorts of colourful marine life; sea turtles, parrotfish, an assortment of rays and what looks like the entire cast of *Finding Nemo* are likely to swim by.

You're going to leave them all behind and drop into the deep.

Divers are encouraged to stay close to the Hole's steep-sided walls, as the descent can be disorientating. There's little to see as you progress. Unlike a 'wall dive', where a sudden drop in the sea bed's elevation can bring all kinds of interesting animals together, there are few living creatures to speak of here.

A HOLE LOT MORE FUN

The Belize coastline is fringed with a succession of low-lying islands, known as 'cayes'. The biggest, most popular launch point for the Blue Hole is Ambergis Caye. It can be a crowded place during peak season but offers lots of lodging options and the best range of charter trips to the Hole. Caye Caulker to the south is smaller but more engaging. You'll have fewer charters to choose from but what you lose in cost you gain in laid-back charm.

Most of your adventures are going to be sea-bound but inland Belize has so much to offer that you really should take a peek. Head for the lush upper section of the Macal River Valley where rippling hills, smothered in bright green forest, spread as far as the eye can see. The trails here incorporate jungle waterfalls, ancient Mayan ruins and, hopefully, some spectacular wildlife sightings. Watch out for vivid scarlet macaws swirling overhead as you cut your way through the foliage.

Divers in the Blue Hole

RAW DETAILS

A Blue Hole dive isn't for novices. You must complete Advanced Open Water diving training before you take the plunge. Courses run by PADI (the Professional Association of Diving Instructors) consist of three main phases:

* Classroom or online study to understand the principles of scuba diving.

* Dives in controlled circumstances and confined water (a swimming pool, in other words) to master basic scuba kills.

* Open water dives, accompanied by an instructor, to apply what you've learned and acquire new skills.

You'll need to familiarize yourself with all sorts of scuba paraphernalia, including using a regulator, a buoyancy control device and your breathing apparatus. The more time you can devote to training, the better. You'll also need to build up your experience of diving to depths of up to 140 feet, which is pretty much the limit for recreational divers. And just as much experience is required in coming back up, obviously.

Things start to get interesting once you reach about 90 ft below sea level.

It's noticeably colder at this depth and most of the colour of the surface has been sucked away. You forget that the sun is blazing in the sky above you. It looks and feels like dusk down here. You're also getting the woozy feeling in your head that comes from sucking hard on high pressure gas. Its Sunday name is 'nitrogen narcosis' and it's nothing to worry about in the long term. The symptoms – light-headedness and a slight deadening of the senses – will disappear as soon as you return to sea level and resume breathing as nature intended, but for now they add to the otherworldly feel of the dive. Some people even find the effect quite pleasing.

You keep dropping down and, with the depth gauge on your wrist reading 130 ft, you find yourself in an underwater lair of eerie beauty. Huge needles of stone jut down from overhangs and upwards from the cave floor. They look like the columns of a subterranean cathedral, or the teeth of a giant, fossilized crocodile, depending on your state of mind.

These lumps of stone are, in fact, stalactites and stalagmites. They are a remnant of the time when the Blue Hole was above ground and its landscape was being shaped by gentle trickles of running water over dry stone. To add to the oddness, some of the stalactites sit at skewed angles. The laws of gravity tell us this shouldn't be possible, but scientists now believe the rocks were jiggled about by an earthquake.

Now they are part of a watery underworld that's sometimes a playground for some pretty serious sea life. As you glide in among the rocks

Coral on the Lighthouse Reef

and explore the openings of the caves behind, you might be joined by an inquisitive shark or studiously ignored by a refrigerator-sized grouper going about its business.

Only after a few minutes at this depth do you notice the lack of movement from the water. There is no tidal pull and no current to speak of, just stillness. The waters at this depth are remarkably clear, which further adds to the surreal feeling of being enveloped in the deep. It's a beguiling place.

And then, just as you feel as if you could explore among the stalactites for hours, you get the nod from the dive master. It's time to head back to real life. You ascend slowly and steadily

and return to the sandy shelf where the fun started a mere 30 minutes ago. Your head clears from the effects of the nitrogen and the water around has lost its coolness. You peer down for one last look but there's nothing to see any more. It's been consumed by the deep blue.

Having spent a short time in such a remarkable place, some people feel slightly underwhelmed by their experience. For others, it's love at first sight. Part of the Blue Hole's magic is the way the experience works its way into your mind and your heart. The thrill of descending into the abyss and emerging from it again is one that lives long in the memory.

MORE DARK DIVES

ORDA CAVE, RUSSIA

Pick your way along a snowy path in the middle of the Russian nowhere, carefully negotiate a descent of some ice-covered steps, pop on your scuba gear... and submerse yourself in a world of brilliant white.

This stunning cave network is made special by a mineral called gypsum.

Its pale colour and smooth texture give the place an ethereal feel, which is only emphasized by the unnervingly clear water. Illuminated only by your diving torch, the caves appear ghostly pale and seem to go on forever. While that's not quite true, this underground maze does extend for more than three miles – plenty of space to explore in the eerie quiet.

Manta Ray, Kona, Hawai'i

KONA, HAWAI'I, USA

This sleepy resort on the Big Island's west coast is known for its wonderful nightlife – marine nightlife, that is. When the sun goes down the waters come alive with majestic manta rays. These ocean giants measure up to 18 feet across their wings and move with awesome grace as they feed on the area's plentiful plankton deposits.

This isn't a difficult dive; just find yourself a comfortable spot on the seabed, kick back and enjoy the show. Unlike their shark cousins, rays have a reputation for playfulness. Don't be surprised if one comes along to give you the once-over. There's one golden rule – don't touch. Contact can damage the ray's skin.

LEMBEH STRAITS, INDONESIA

Muck diving: doesn't exactly sound enticing, does it? It's the name given to scuba sojourns in areas that are covered with sand or sediment. The murky waters of the Lembeh Straits, between the islands of Sulawesi and Lembeh, might not boast the ridiculous colours of a tropical reef, but the dull sands house all sorts of weird and wonderful sea creatures who can't wait to make your acquaintance. There are more than 60 dive sites to choose from here so you won't be overrun with fellow divers. Expect to encounter intricate seahorses, freaky-looking frogfish and assorted species of octopus during your dive.

Situated in the eastern foothills of the Ural Mountains, the wonders of Orda were virtually unknown to the world until the fall of the Berlin Wall brought a few hardy visitors, drawn by folk tales of a magical underwater world. Even now, the remote location keeps the masses away. Make the journey and take the dive. You won't regret it.

RUN FOR YOUR LIFE
Ultramarathons

These days, it seems, there's nothing particularly special about doing a marathon. The challenge of pushing your human frame to pound out 26 miles and 385 yards is certainly not to be sniffed at, but it's no longer the preserve of an elite few. Each year tens of thousands of runners take part in events in cities such as New York, Mumbai, London and Tokyo.

Many of them are in great shape and post worthy times. But thousands more complete the race wearing tuxedos, joined together inside a comedy horse or hopping backwards while singing Bob Dylan songs. They're doing it for charity, of course, and that's generous and noble and to be applauded. But the point is that the marathon simply doesn't have the cachet it once had of being 'A Really Long Race'. So what's a hardcore distance runner to do?

Go further, that's what.

Ultramarathons – events run over a course far longer than the standard 26 miles – are booming in popularity. High-profile events like the Marathon de Sables in the Sahara Desert sell out in minutes. Races over 50 or even 100 miles are popping up all over the place. These new, more extreme, events invite entrants to try interesting new ways of pushing their body to the limit... and way, way beyond.

THE BARKLEY MARATHONS, FROZEN HEAD STATE PARK, TENNESSEE, USA

DIFFICULTY **★★★★**★

ENDURANCE **★★★★★**

NERVES OF STEEL **★★★**★★

DURATION: 60 HOURS IF YOU
FINISH ALL FIVE LOOPS

PERSONNEL: 40 ENTRANTS PER YEAR

SKILLSET: ENDURANCE AND THEN SOME

RISKS: DEHYDRATION, DISORIENTATION, HALLUCINATIONS,
EXTREME EXHAUSTION, SHREDDED FEET & LEGS

An endurance race like no other; the eccentric Barkley Marathons will take you to the limit – and that's just the 'warm-up' loop over the first 12 hours. With five loops in total, through snake-infested Tennessee wilderness, it's no wonder, in most years, no one finishes at all.

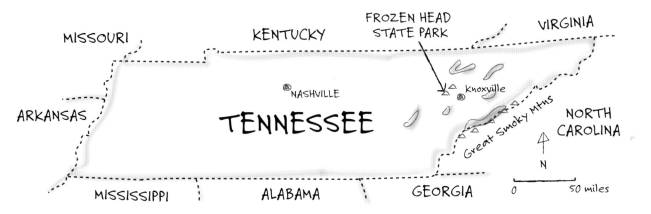

First rule of Barkley Marathons: don't talk about Barkley Marathons.

This most enigmatic of ultra events takes place in the wild woods of backcountry Tennessee and the route changes more or less every year. That's about as much as anyone will tell you. "There is an understanding that people aren't going to talk about it," says former contestant

Seth Wolgin. "It's supposed to be a learning experience; you're not supposed to finish it the first time."

Few endurance events are shrouded in as much mystery as the Barkley Marathons. The application process is harder than getting in to Hogwarts. Competitors must send their application to a secret email address at a

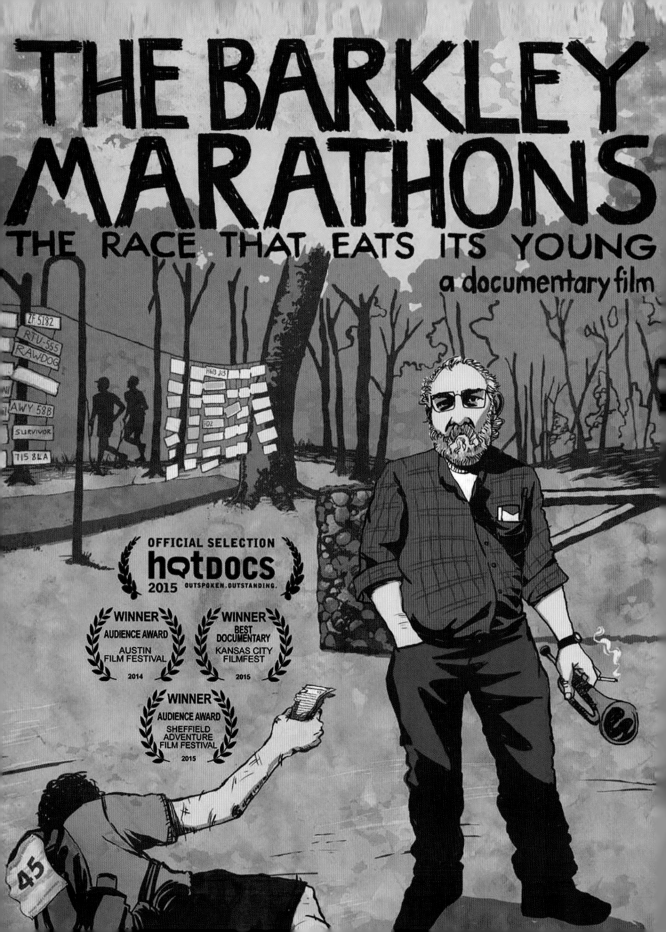

specific time. This information isn't advertised. Wannabees need to turn detective and infiltrate the Barkley Marathons community. If you apply five minutes too late, it's game over for another year.

Applicants must also supply a personal essay pleading their case and complete a bizarre, unrelated written examination. Hundreds apply despite the difficulties but only 40 will receive a letter of condolence:

"It is my unfortunate duty to inform you that your name has been selected for the Barkley Marathons."

Each year one 'sacrificial lamb' is allowed to run. This competitor has absolutely no chance of completing the race and has no business being out there. This lamb to the slaughter will typically last just five or six hours. Why allow someone who has no chance of success to compete? For the hell of it, that's why. Understand that and you're on your way to getting a handle on the bonkers world of the Barkley Marathons.

The cold, hard reality is that most people quit – 98.5 percent of starters won't finish the race. Only 15 competitors have ever completed the course out of the thousand or so who've tried over the years. When someone quits, a bugler plays 'Taps' to let everyone in the valley know another poor soul has bitten the dust.

A RACE FOR FOOLS IN APRIL

Competitors must complete five 20-mile loops within 60 hours, on a course that changes every year. That's a total of 100 miles through the toughest, gnarliest terrain of any ultramarathon – often in wild weather. Most long distance races take place on a nice, smooth bit of asphalt. This race is run over dirt, mud, running water and solid rock. There are sudden drops and rocky crags to climb. This is countryside as a weapon.

B.M. ECCENTRICITIES

* The application costs $1.60. No one gets a refund.

* There is no trophy or prize money, just legendary status.

* The rules are harsh and strictly enforced as Canadian Gary Robbins discovered in 2017. While in second place on Loop Five he took a wrong turn on the final descent, costing him precious time. He reached the finish just six seconds over the 60-hour-mark only to be marked as a DNF.

* Record for Futility. The slowest competitor ever was 75-year-old Dan Baglione who lasted 32 hours but completed just two miles.

* Many of the hills and landmarks have been given their own unofficial names over the years, such as Rat Jaw, Son of a Bitch Ditch, Pillars of Doom and Leonard's Butt Slide – the latter named after a guy who tried and failed multiple times to complete the course.

* Over the course of 60 hours, those who finish climb and descend the equivalent of Mount Everest twice.

The walk off

RACE ORIGINS

In 1977, James Earl Ray, the man who killed Martin Luther King Jnr, escaped from Brushy Mountain State Penitentiary along with five other inmates. After 50 hours and a state-wide manhunt Ray was still on the loose. Many thought he was well on his way to Mexico. The locals weren't convinced. They knew how tough the terrain was and renewed their search of the immediate area. He was eventually found in Frozen Head State Park, lying utterly exhausted, just eight miles from the prison.

Gary Cantrell (a.k.a. Lazarus Lake or just Laz) and Karl Henn (a.k.a. Raw Dog), decided to find out why this escaped murderer had covered so few miles when his freedom was at stake. Although highly experienced long-distance runners themselves, they found the off-piste terrain much tougher than expected. Naming it after a friend who was injured during the Vietnam war, the duo founded the Barkley Marathons and the first race was run in 1986. It's been hell ever since.

There are no markers, no marshals, no food stops, no first aiders and only two water points. It's an old-school extravaganza so GPS devices and altimeters are strictly forbidden. A map and compass, that's it.

Except you are not really given a course map. A map of the route is made available just before the race starts but competitors don't get to keep it. Instead, they have to copy the route onto their own map and use the directions provided. This is to force everyone to get a handle on the terrain before they start. Unfortunately, these 'directions' are a bit vague:

"Keep on following the ridge up to the highest point, when it hurts more you are on the right path..."

Experience is everything when it comes to deciphering the clues.

Around a dozen or so books are placed around the course to ensure there is no cheating. Runners must tear out the page which corresponds to their race number to prove they made it all the way round. As a reminder of the pain you're in – as if you could forget – the books have apt titles: *A Time to Die*, *Alone and Helpless* and *Death Walk in the Woods* being charming examples.

The race can start at any time between midnight and noon on the nearest Saturday to April Fools' day. A ceremonial conch shell is blown, after which the competitors have one hour to prepare. No one knows when the conch will sound; few sleep well in their tents that night. As a result, most are tired before the race even starts. All part of the test.

There's no huge fanfare to signal it's time for the misery to begin. A race organizer nicknamed Lazarus lights a cigarette and the competitors walk away until they are out of his sight. This

eccentric tradition is to avoid giving Lazarus the satisfaction of seeing everyone scuttle off as if they're in a hurry.

Laz signals for the race to start

By the time 12 hours are up and the exhausted competitors have completed Loop One, one third will have dropped out. After only a short break, and with darkness falling, it's time for Loop Two. Competitors are at least allowed a head torch for the all-nighter through the sticks. The bugler is a busy man around this time. By the end of this loop, the field will have been shredded by a further two-thirds. Hardy athletes, unaccustomed to failure, lie in crumpled heaps around the campsite – broken both physically and mentally.

"The ambition for many is to just be a regular failure and not a miserable one."

THE FUN RUN

For the remaining competitors, Loop Three, or the 'Fun Run' as it's ironically called, awaits. Completing the third loop is the primary goal for most. But remember, we're barely over the halfway point in this race from hell. Up until now it's not really been a race at all. Barkley Marathons virgins tend to stick with the vets who are usually pleased to help anyone who

VIRGINS

Barkley Marathons virgins, as they are known, must bring a car license plate from whichever state or country they are from. These are hung around the campsite during the race. Vets are requested to bring a specified item of clothing for Laz. White shirts, until he had too many, socks until he had too many and so on. Previous finishers have to bring a packet of smokes for Laz.

"If you are going to face a real challenge, it has to be a REAL challenge, you can't accomplish anything without the possibility of failure."
Gary 'Lazarus' Cantrell

HOW THE BARKLEY BEATS YOU UP

Most entrants are already experienced ultramarathon competitors so why do few Barkley Marathons competitors last the course? Here are a few factors:

* Terrain – the route changes every year but always adds up to 100 miles of going up, down and across treacherously steep ravines.

* Water – competitors have to wade through stagnant ponds and free-flowing rivers.

* Weather – hot days and freezing cold nights.

* Thorns – jagged spikes everywhere.

* Mud – trying to run through patches of cloying Tennessee mud saps energy and kills momentum.

* Woods – constantly hacking through dense foliage drains your strength.

* Brain freeze – a total lack of landmarks means it's all too easy to get lost in the woods.

* Fatigue – all of the above factors are made so much worse by the fact you'll be exhausted.

The smiles won't last

needs assistance. It's a collective effort to beat the course for as long as possible.

Assuming anyone is left, it becomes a proper race on Loop Four. Chances are that 95 percent of the competitors are now back at camp wondering if they'll ever walk again, never mind run. Those left need to think carefully whether or not to head off into the night once more – quitting while on the course could still leave them with up to a 10-hour walk back to their tent. Deprived of sleep for two days, it's not uncommon for competitors to start hallucinating, and many are found wandering around aimlessly in the woods, mumbling incoherently.

Until 1995, some 10 years after the first race, no one had completed Loop Five. It was thought impossible and the 'Fun Run' was generally regarded as the main event. Once Englishman Mark Williams became the first person to

complete the race, a mental barrier was broken – this crazy challenge was do-able after all. But this success didn't go unpunished and the following year the course was toughened up. Six years would pass before it would be completed again. And again the course was made harder the following year.

Why create a race that only a fraction of competitors will ever finish? Lazarus insists that it's not about him revelling in other people's misery – mostly! Instead, because everyone knows the bugler will eventually serenade them, it's up to the competitors to find their own personal breaking point. That's the whole idea.

One thing's for certain, there is no other race quite like the Barkley Marathons.

BLOOD, SWEAT & TEARS – MORE LONG RUNS

JUNGLE ULTRA, PERU

During Peru's Jungle Ultra it's not just other competitors you need to concern yourself with. To add a bit more spice to the week-long summer race you'll be sharing the remote terrain with a huge variety of wildlife including monkeys, jaguars, snakes and biting ants. It starts at 10,000 feet, up in the Cloud Forest, before descending to the dense virgin jungle below. Humidity levels reach 100 percent so sweating won't cool you as you traverse 143 tropical miles of mud, rivers and mountain paths. The local tribespeople will look on with amusement as you pass by their villages in what seems like an utterly pointless expenditure of energy.

MARATHON DES SABLES, MOROCCO

1,300 competitors; five-and-a-half marathons in as many days; the Sahara Desert in southern Morocco; temperatures exceeding 120°F. Advice: carry plenty of water. What else do you need to know? Or, if you fancy something more palatable that's just a short flight from Europe, try

Marathon des Sables

the NOMAD'S RUN near Marrakesh. It's a mere 50 miles long, with 10 percent of the profits going to the local community. There are some short races tagged on so you can even bring the kids!

YUKON ARCTIC ULTRA, CANADA

You can elect to race the 100-mile, 300-mile or 430-mile marathon distance in the coldest ultra in the world. The race takes place in mid-winter and temperatures can drop to -40°F so there is a risk of frostbite. You can choose your mode of discipline: cross country skis, mountain bike or foot.

SPARTATHALON, GREECE

Following in the footsteps of Pheidippides, an ancient Athenian courier, this 153-mile ultramarathon takes place in September each year. According to Greek history, Pheidippides ran from Athens to Sparta in a day and a half to seek help while the Greeks were at war with the Persians. The modern race dates from 1983, the year after five RAF officers tried to see if they could run the route within the same timeframe.

"Aboriginal Australians believe the brain is just an analytical tool, everything should come from the gut. We should rely less on our mind and more on our instincts."

FOUR LEGS GOOD, TWO LEGS BAD

Walking with animals

There are some corners of our planet where human beings just aren't meant to go. Searing hot deserts, freezing icefields and rock-strewn high plains being prime examples. These epic, inhospitable landscapes put pressures on our bodies that they weren't built to cope with for any real length of time. And yet the very fact that Mother Nature has posted a giant 'keep out' sign on these places makes them somehow even more alluring.

Fortunately, she has been far more accommodating to other species. Many animals are infinitely better equipped than we are to handle extreme environments. Working with beasts that can bear the burdens we can't makes it possible to take a glimpse at remote regions where few people dare to tread. But, be warned, relying on a living, breathing creature to get you and your kit through the wilderness is fraught with difficulty. You'll have to keep your wits about you if you want to work with animals in the wilderness... and make it back to tell the tale.

CAMEL TREKKING, DANAKIL DESERT, NORTHEAST AFRICA

Descend into one of the hottest places on Earth – the fearsome Danakil Depression in northern Ethiopia. Here you'll slowly roast in temperatures in excess of 120°F (50°C) as you walk along spectacular salt flats and past eerie tribal burial grounds. Your only friends? Two camels, carrying life-saving provisions through this searing high-temperature challenge.

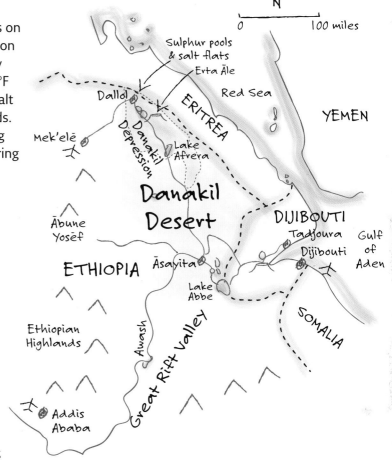

DIFFICULTY   ★★★★★
ENDURANCE   ★★★★☆
NERVES OF STEEL ★★★☆☆

DURATION: 10-14 DAYS
PERSONNEL: YOU, PLUS TWO CAMELS
SKILLSET: CAMEL WRANGLING, NAVIGATION, SHELTER-BUILDING
RISKS: SUNSTROKE, DEHYDRATION

In other circumstances, the bizarre situation in which you find yourself would actually be quite funny. You're trotting along behind a very grumpy runaway camel, begging it to stop so that you can rope it in and resume your journey. You've been taught various camel commands and have tried them all – plus a few, more colourful, expressions of your own – but this awkward bugger is turning a deaf ear to your increasingly desperate cries. You've tried looping round to get in front of it; you've tried staring it down; you've tried sneaking up from behind. Every time you almost get close enough to make a grab for its reins, the big beast jogs away again, staying tantalizingly beyond your reach.

So, yes, this would be reasonably amusing in a different time and place. But in the here-and-

Camel train carrying salt through the Danakil

now, in the relentless heat of the world's hottest desert, it's not funny at all. It's deadly serious. You've already wasted an hour running about trying to regain control of the situation. You can't afford to quit. The camel you're chasing has most of your fresh drinking water and the tarpaulin you need to shield you from the sun when you rest. Without these things, it won't take very long for the heat to claim you. You could die if you don't catch that camel.

Eventually, gloriously, your four-legged 'friend' has had enough and allows you to get close enough to wrangle it back under control. You're too relieved to be angry. That was close, and you've got nobody to blame for this brush with disaster but yourself. One of the clearest instructions you'd been given was to never, under any circumstances, stop checking on your camels. You lost focus and in the blink of an eye the camel had bitten through its rope and decided to go for a wander. You are lucky it decided not to wander too far. And now you find you've had

another stroke of luck, the other camel, which is carrying the rest of your water, most of your food and your medical kit, is pretty much where you left it.

Order is restored. You can get back on the trail.

'A LAND OF DEATH'

The Danakil Desert, which covers roughly 140,000 square miles of Ethiopia, Djibouti and Eritrea, is an interesting place for all sorts of reasons. It's punishingly hot and features landscapes that look more like the surface of another planet than anywhere on Earth. There are vast salt pans that shimmer in the sun, craters of bubbling lava and mineral-rich hydro-thermal lakes that boil in violent shades of red and green and stink of sulphur. The legendary explorer Wilfred Thesiger, who knew a thing or two about tough desert conditions, called this area 'a land of death'.

Slap-bang in the middle of this odd landscape sits the Danakil Depression, which is even more punishing and inhospitable than its surrounding environs. The Depression is 300 ft below sea level and some of the hottest temperatures on Earth have been recorded in this sunken cauldron.

And yet, despite all this, some still call it home. The Afar people have lived and worked on this scorched earth for hundreds, perhaps thousands, of years. Even in the 21st century, many Afar still live as nomadic herdsmen, roaming through the heat with herds of cattle and goat. They also head into the heart of the desert to mine the region's most precious commodity – salt. Huge deposits of the stuff can be found here, creating a dazzling white surface across wide swathes of country. It's a surreal experience to look across vast salt flats. For all the world it looks like snowfall.

Salt mining is an important source of income for the Afar and other inhabitants of this area. They head out into the badlands and hack up huge chunks of the stuff, which are wrapped up in slabs and taken to market. None of the salt-gathering would be possible without one of nature's unsung heroes (and occasionally troublesome travel companions) - the camel. These beasts of burden are vital to human activity here. It's camels that you'll need if you want to venture out into the Danakil Depression and test yourself in the burning zone.

MOSTLY CONCERNING CAMELS

There is much to admire about camels. They can withstand the worst the desert has to throw at them, plodding along for days on end with a heavy load on their back and never a need to be fed or watered. That said, they aren't the

CAMEL BUSINESS

Sometimes the greatest attribute you can have when setting out on a hardcore expedition is a bit of humility. Acquiring a couple of camels in the area around Mek'elē isn't particularly difficult. Knowing how to handle them, however, is extremely difficult. You're going to need guidance, which means asking for help from people who are richly experienced in working with camels in the Danakil - the Afar. So much of how we travel nowadays can be done digitally. In many ways that's a huge step forward but sometimes it obscures one of the deepest benefits that should be part of any big adventure, which is the opportunity to connect with humans from totally different backgrounds and cultures. A journey into the Danakil should be a once-in-a-lifetime experience and would be incomplete without getting some insight into the remarkable people who inhabit the area. So go out on a limb, be humble, and find people who live in the landscape and ask them for help. It's the proper way to start your adventure.

most endearing travel companions. They fart constantly, are prone to biting and sometimes they just don't want to play ball. Learning how to work with your camels is one of the most critical factors in a successful journey.

The city of Mek'elē is a decent starting point for your adventure. Here you should be able to stock up on supplies, source some camels and find someone who can give you training in how to handle them. Once you've mastered the basic commands – and all the commands are all pretty basic; camels don't do subtle nuance – you are ready to descend into the Depression. There are a few roads heading east from here and it makes sense to stay close to them in the early stages of your trek. Partly because it's easier ground to walk over and there's no point punishing the soles of your feet at this stage but also because it gives you a chance to put in a few hours with your camels and build a respectful working relationship, even if it is likely to be a bit grudging on the camels' part.

Unless you are desperate to know what it feels like to be a roast dinner, you should aim to spend no more than two nights and three days in the Depression itself – time enough to get a feel for the place without doing any lasting damage to your body.

Aim to make your mileage in the same way the Afar do. Get up before sunrise and walk in the early mornings; bring a canvas sheet or tarpaulin to hole up out of the sun during the heat of the day and walk some more in the late afternoon and early evenings before making camp for the night.

It's difficult to come to terms with the landscape here. Some deserts – like the soaring sand dunes of the Namib in southern Africa or the soft, red-coloured arches of Moab in the USA – can be places of real beauty. Danakil isn't beautiful. The scenery confronts you in a way that's almost hostile. You'll walk across miles of sharp rock only to come face-to-face with sights so bizarre your mind struggles to process them. There are ponds discoloured by chemicals that turn the water blood red; garish yellow salt formations that look like flowers in bloom; narrow fissures in the earth that spew out noxious-smelling gases in shimmering plumes. It might not be pretty, but it's absolutely fascinating.

FIRE & BRIMSTONE

Your route is yours to choose but there are some sights you shouldn't miss. At Dallol, the sulphur and iron oxide spewing from the ground has created gnarly columns of garish greens and yellows. The colours and heat combine to create a searingly intense landscape that only exists in this sunken pocket of the world. The other main stop should be Irta'ale Volcano. As peaks go, it's no biggie, just 2,000 ft above sea level but, when your ascent starts below sea level and is carried out in oven-grade heat, it certainly feels high enough. Make your climb at night to avoid the glare of the sun. Take a torch – and a jacket; it can get a little chilly at night, believe it or not. Your reward for reaching the rim is a gurgling crater of lava that's been constantly erupting in its own low-key way for more than 50 years.

You never get used to the burning temperatures or the sulphurous stench of this remarkable country, but you do learn to accommodate them, even if it is only for a few days. The sense of freedom you'll get from roaming this wilderness and experiencing some of Earth's most unusual natural wonders is pretty special. Just make sure you keep an eye on those bloody camels.

Dallol Lake

BORDER PROBLEMS

The Danakil desert spans the border between Ethiopia, Eritrea and Djibouti. At the time of publication the border between Ethiopia and Eritrea was firmly shut amid tensions between the two countries. All the areas mentioned in this description of Danakil are found in the Afar region of Ethiopia and any attempt to extend your expedition by crossing the border into Eritrea would be a very bad idea indeed.

The United Kingdom Foreign Office advises caution when travelling in Afar and recommends using a recognized tour company, who will normally provide armed support during your stay. Don't let this advice put you off – a decent tour operator will buy into what you're trying to do and can help as much as possible to make it happen. Just be clear on what you want and find a firm that shares your passion.

ANIMAL POWER

HUSKIES, GREENLAND

If you've never coasted through a snowy mountain valley with the rear ends of half-a-dozen dogs bouncing purposefully in front of you, well, you've never really lived. The Inuit people of eastern Greenland have been using dog sleds to navigate the massive Arctic expanses for centuries. An expedition here using packs of huskies is an opportunity to explore a landscape of snow and ice that's largely unknown other than to a small number of indigenous people. You'll trace a trail alongside, and sometimes over, frozen fjords on your way to traditional villages and hunting grounds. Along the way you'll encounter jagged icebergs rising violently out of the sea and, hopefully, some of the region's surprisingly rich animal life. Learning how to handle your own sled takes years of practical experience but you'll have an opportunity to join in and get to grips with some of the basics.

CATTLE DRIVING, USA

If you fancy your chances of being a modern-day John Wayne or Calamity Jane, there are hundreds of options for taking part in a cattle drive in the American West. Proceed with caution. Some packages have more in common with a Florida theme park than the Wild West, so it pays to do your research before you go. Get it right, however, and time spent on horseback on the raw, rugged range can be hugely rewarding. The real thing will be too much hard work to feel like a holiday. You'll be expected to muck in with the unglamorous side of cattle-wrangling and, despite what the movies might show, the weather out West isn't always warm and sunny. For all that, a properly run cattle drive will give you a chance to live out under the stars as you guide cattle across open country.

Husky sledding tour,
Tasiilaq, Greenland

BEEKEEPING, SLOVENIA

You've coerced camels in the desert, handled huskies across snowfields and wrangled horses on the prairie – how about a change of pace? The tiny eastern European nation of Slovenia loves bees. There are an estimated 90,000 beekeepers, which is impressive in a country of just two million people. Slovenians are rightly proud of the indigenous Carniolan honey bee which is renowned for its non-aggressive nature and distinctive-tasting honey. A few days among the hives in Slovenia's Alpine countryside is an almost meditative experience. Perhaps you'll enjoy it so much, by the time you return home, you'll think about doing it yourself. You may not make a fortune, but the local flowers will be grateful.

WALK THE WORLD
Long-distance hiking

There's a massive difference between walking a trail for a couple of weeks and embarking on a heavy-duty trek. On a long expedition you won't see home for many months. Your feet, legs, back – every bone in your body in fact – will slowly feel like they are breaking down. It's not just a physical test, it's a psychological challenge, too. It can change your outlook on life – that's often the main reason why people undertake such a gruelling endeavour. But there is another attraction... simplicity.

You can get started with just the basics: backpack, map, compass, water bottle, sleeping bag, tent and boots. Preferably a very, very comfortable pair of boots. You don't have to be super fit, just in good enough shape to walk for a few days, knowing your conditioning will improve as you go.

What you do need is resilience, commitment and determination to keep going day after day after day for a thousand miles or more.

Once you are done, you may never wish to put your battered and bruised feet into a pair of hiking boots again, but you'll be a different person. Your view of yourself, and the world around you, will be forever altered.

THE PACIFIC CREST TRAIL, WESTERN USA

The Pacific Crest Trail or PCT, as it's commonly known, is the mother of all long-distance trails. On its way northbound it passes through just about every climate zone the western United States has to offer. From warm, waterless desert on the Mexican border through to rain-soaked northern Washington – the PCT has it all.

DIFFICULTY **★★★**✩✩

ENDURANCE **★★★★★**

NERVES OF STEEL **★★**✩✩✩

DURATION: 5 MONTHS APPROX.

PERSONNEL: SOLO OR SMALL GROUP

SKILLSET: ENDURANCE, DETERMINATION

RISKS: HEAT EXHAUSTION, DEHYDRATION, RATTLESNAKES, BEARS, AVALANCHES

Two thousand, six hundred and fifty miles. Even the words are daunting. It's an almost unimaginable amount of ground to cover in one continuous hike. A journey on such a scale pushes you to the limit: mentally, physically and financially. Your life is on hold until you achieve the holy grail or give up trying.

Yet, every year, a few hundred hikers complete the PCT. Others do it in sections, returning annually until the job is done. Many try but only a small percentage of hardy individuals complete all of it.

Forgetting the point-to-point distance for a moment, it's also a monumental collection of ups and downs. If you walk the full PCT you have to climb 489,000 ft. And with an overall elevation gain of 1,000 ft – assuming you are hiking north – what goes up must come down. The 488,000-ft descent is the equivalent of dropping down to the bottom of the Mariana Trench in the Pacific Ocean, not once, but thirteen times over. Mind blowing? Yes. Exciting? Definitely.

The PCT was one of America's first National Scenic Trails. Along with its more famous cousin, the Appalachian Trail on the other side of America, it was opened in 1968. However, it wasn't until 1993 that it was officially declared complete. It passes through four National Monuments, five State Parks, 26 National Forests and seven National Parks. Not a bad haul for five months of blood, sweat and tears.

Virtually all through-hikers head north, following the seasons. With this in mind, the PCT starts for most in spring on the Mexican border at Campo. From there it weaves its way to Canada broadly following the higher parts of the Sierra Nevada and Cascade mountain ranges. In southern California it first goes through the Anza Borrego desert where it's not uncommon to see the border patrol helicopters carrying out their daily routines to remind you how far south you are. From there the trail climbs 7,500 ft up to Mount San Jacinto leaving the desert behind and entering a landscape of pine forests and snowmelt creeks.

That's the first serious climb under your belt – just another 50 or so like that to go. You'll need to make sure you stock up on water because the trail then drops back to the desert floor. It's a slog through the waterless Mojave Desert. Right about now you'll question the wisdom of your decision to make this trip, especially when you stumble upon your first rattlesnake on the trail.

Assuming you've given yourself a talking to, yelled a bit, kicked a few rocks around and controlled your temper tantrums, it's time to head for Kennedy Meadows, the gateway to the Sierra Nevada, where you can rest up for a few days and share stories with fellow hikers. It'll feel like paradise.

PACIFIC CREST TRAIL CROSS SECTION

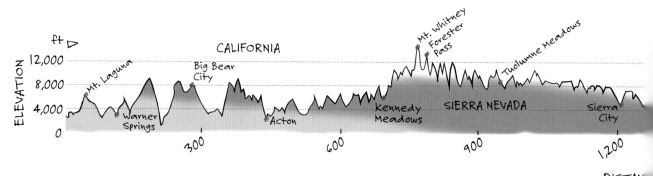

ROOKIE ERRORS TO AVOID... on long-distance hikes

* Make sure you have a valid visa for your extended stay for all the countries you'll visit. You won't be able to renew it when you're halfway up a mountain pass.

* Get used to carrying a large backpack before you start and be sure to wear in your hiking boots. If there's the slightest niggling doubt that something isn't quite right, fix the problem. Almost certainly, 100 miles in, that niggle could destroy your walk. Boots that are slightly too big allow for your feet to swell – if they are too small, you've screwed.

* Buy quality gear and essentials only. Pack light, but be realistic about what you'll need. Send supplies ahead of you to collect on the way.

"Thousands of tired, nerve-shaken, over-civilized people are beginning to find out that going to the mountains is going home; that wildness is a necessity; and that mountain parks and reservations are useful not only as fountains of timber and irrigating rivers, but as fountains of life."
John Muir

TOTAL ELEVATION GAIN: 1,000 FT
489,500 FT OF CLIMBING AND 488,500 FT DESCENDING

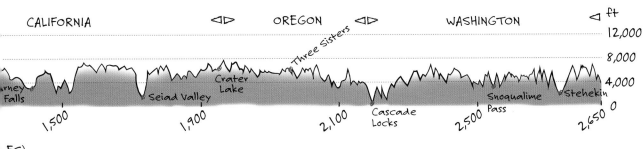

GO SOLO OR WITH A FRIEND?

Many people do long-distance hikes alone but let's be honest, providing your buddy doesn't drive you crazy every step of the way, it's much more fun to hike with a mate – and safer. If you don't have someone in mind, there are plenty of online hiking groups, and a few are focussed on the PCT specifically. If you are intent on hiking with someone, it's best to organize this beforehand. You'll meet lots of people on the trail, some of whom you'll hook up with for several days, but it's a risk to assume you'll end up doing the whole route with them.

JOHN MUIR TRAIL

As you depart for the Sierra Nevada you are now following in the footsteps of the granddaddy of America naturalism, John Muir, first into Sequoia National Park, then Kings Canyon before entering Muir's back yard, Yosemite.

When it reaches the Sierra Nevada, the PCT overlaps with the John Muir Trail (JMT), and for many, this 211-mile section is the highlight of the whole journey. It passes through wild, beautiful mountain scenery – maybe the most spectacular in the United States. With pine forests as far as the eye can see, a thousand shimmering lakes and towering peaks that reach 14,000 ft, it feels like a compilation of the PCT's greatest hits. If you can't commit to the whole PCT but still long for a truly great wilderness experience in America's West, put the JMT on your bucket list.

There are all sorts of tempting detours to make here, including the awe-inspiring Yosemite valley, but if you stick to the PCT you're about to hit a high point – literally. The trail takes you through eight passes over 11,000 ft. At 13,200 ft, Forester Pass is as close to the sky as you'll get; make the most of it by taking a refreshing swim in one of the natural pools near the path.

The PCT skirts by Lake Tahoe and its casinos before turning west towards Mount Shasta. By the time it reaches the Cascade Range in southern Oregon, 1,600 miles are on the clock. Your body will be stronger and your mind will have relaxed into the rhythm of life on the trail by now. Or there's a small chance it will be broken. The simplicity of putting one foot in front of another will make you realize that you are no longer on holiday from your distant, 'civilized' world. The PCT has become your life.

Although the PCT is a marked trail, it can't be mistaken for a motorway. There are many unsigned intersections – stay vigilant or you'll end up going off in totally the wrong direction. The terrain varies enormously and markers are often difficult to find, especially in bad weather. In heavy snow, staying on the trail is virtually impossible unless you are a highly experienced navigator. Another factor you'll need to consider when you are taking compass bearings on your map, is that because the trail is so long, there is a big variation in the magnetic declination.

JOHN MUIR

Muir, a Scottish immigrant, made the Sierra Nevada his home during the second half of the 19th century, often spending long periods alone in the wilderness. He popularized a radically new concept of American land use and conservation. His writings moved presidents, congressmen, and ordinary Americans to action.

Famously, Theodore Roosevelt, who was seeking re-election for the presidency, visited Muir in Yosemite and the two of them spent three days camping in the valley, hiking and talking. Following his re-election in 1904, Roosevelt set aside well over 300,000 square miles of national parks across the nation.

Alpine Lakes Wilderness, Cascade Mountains

THE CASCADES

As you leave California and the Sierra Nevada behind, you reach the Cascade Range which extends 700 miles up into British Columbia in Canada. It'll now be late summer and wild fires are a real danger. You may walk through charred forests for dozens of miles and struggle to take a breath of fresh air. However, your mood will be lifted when you see the new shoots of life sprouting from the ash on the forest floor.

Oregon means Crater Lake and the Three Sisters Wilderness – a land of glaciers and volcanic landscapes full of bubbling springs, cinder cones and lava flows. Next you'll pass Mount Hood, Oregon's highest peak and a dormant volcano. It's predicted to erupt sometime this century. So, with a bit of luck, you might get to witness a free fireworks display!

Your journey becomes a battle against time as you enter Washington State. Winter is fast approaching and the race is on to reach the Canadian border before the weather starts to bite in the wet climate of the Northern Cascades. With mist-covered mountains all around you, a part of you will be desperate to finish, the other will sense a sadness with the knowledge that your five-month escape from the modern world and all its trappings is drawing to a close.

OTHER 'STROLLS' TO CONSIDER

GR10, FRANCE

Often overshadowed by the Alps, the Pyrenees are not to be sniffed at. These are serious mountains but they invite rather than intimidate the average hiker, plus, they are much less crowded. There are three main routes across the Pyrenees, all worthy of consideration, but the GR10 is probably the pick of the bunch. Although it hugs the French–Spanish border, almost all of this 538-mile hike lies within France. It begins in Hendaye on the Atlantic coast and finishes in Banyuls-Sur-Mer on the

Mediterranean Sea. The GR10 takes you through some of the most rugged and wild landscapes in Western Europe. It passes through farmland, lakes, high mountain passes and traditional picture-perfect French villages and can usually be completed in about five to seven weeks.

GREAT WALL OF CHINA: ALL OF IT!

Yes, you can book a two-week walking holiday and have everything taken care of but where's the fun in that? What most people don't realize is that it's possible to walk the whole 4,000 miles across northern

Ilhéou's refuge
GR10, France

China. Start in Yumenguan in Gansu province and end at Tiger Mountain close to the North Korean border. Very few people have completed the Wall Walk in its entirety and there are many sections that require detours. It's incredibly steep in places but at least you don't have to worry too much about losing sight of the path.

GREATER PATAGONIA TRAIL, S. AMERICA

If you fancy being a trailblazer, this is the one for you. The GPT is 1,300 miles long but the 'path' is very much a work-in-progress – it's a bit like the PCT as it was in its early days. There are no reassuring route markers as it's really just a series of vaguely connected trails, roads and dirt tracks. Only a handful of hardy souls have completed the route which begins near Chile's capital Santiago and runs south through some of the wildest, most rugged and jaw-dropping scenery on Earth. The ultimate goal is to extend the route by another 700 miles all the way to Tierra Del Fuego.

THE QUEST FOR ENLIGHTENMENT

Spiritual growth

Why are you reading this book? What is it that you want to achieve? Do you seek glory? Exhilaration? Or, by challenging yourself, do you want to get to know the real you? To discover all that you can be and, perhaps more importantly, accept that which you cannot? To find your place in the world? In the cosmos, even?

In contrast to the great explorers and adventurers, there are people who would say that the greatest rewards are found on a very different sort of journey. Peace, enlightenment, total confidence, supreme physical strength, joy – all these can be be found by adventuring within yourself.

LIVE LIKE A MONK, WU WEI SI MONASTERY, YUNNAN PROVINCE, CHINA

Open your mind and nourish your soul by giving up your old life to what is arguably a greater test of mental and physical strength than all the other adventures in this book combined. The rewards, however, will set your mind free.

DIFFICULTY **★★★★**★

ENDURANCE **★★★★★**

NERVES OF STEEL **★★**★★★

DURATION: 7 YEARS
PERSONNEL: JUST YOU
SKILLSET: SELF-DISCIPLINE, HUMILITY, DEDICATION
RISKS: LONELINESS, INJURY, FAILURE

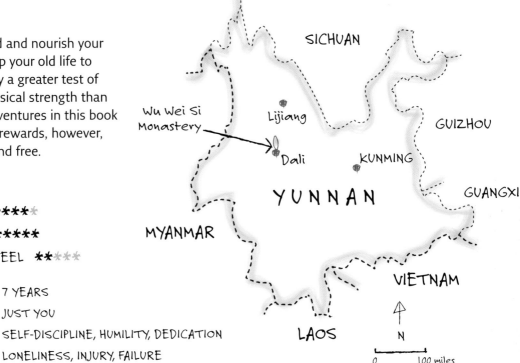

Pick up the iron bar. Heft it. Feel its weight. The hardness. Now focus hard and smash it into pieces over your head. It is clearly an absurd and impossible task. But you are prepared. You are supremely fit and strong – far more athletic than most of the people who climb Mount Everest will ever be. You are as supple as a gymnast, as powerful as a boxer and as deadly as a ninja. Plus, you have something even more special: a serene inner confidence and mental clarity born of thousands of hours of meditation. These abilities give you the power to perform feats that look near-superhuman to ordinary people. That iron bar is history...

FIND YOURSELF IN THE MIDDLE OF NOWHERE

They don't know you're coming, or why, or even who you are. This is partly because this is a monastic temple, where the ego is shed and all focus is on the infinite power of the Other. But it's also because they don't have a phone.

Tiger Leaping Gorge
near Lijiang

Or, for that matter, an email address or website. Welcome to Wu Wei Si Monastery, in Yunnan province, southern China.

It is everything you hoped a Shaolin temple would be. Reached by rickety cab ride from an ancient market town, the temple nestles on a forested mountainside with a shimmering blue lake nearby. The blood-red buildings are capped with gently curving, tiled roofs. An entrance gate is supported by grotesque carved statues. This takes you into a square inner yard dotted with bamboo shrubs where yellow-clad monks exercise in unison as incense smoke blues the air and tingles your nostrils.

You are here because, unusually for a Shaolin temple, Wu Wei Si welcomes foreigners and offers them training in the ancient art of Shaolin kung fu. For the next few weeks, you will live with the monks and do as they do. You will rise at 5 am to pray for an hour before beginning training at six. This starts with a swift run to a boulder-strewn river. There you must pick up

DO OR DIE

In the last two centuries, only 46 men have finished the Kaihogyo. This is a challenge you have to take very, very seriously. Once a monk has run his first 100 days he is committed – tradition says he must now complete the challenge or take his own life. As he runs he always carries with him a short sword. The mountainside around the monastery is peppered with unmarked graves.

the largest rock you can and carry it back to the monastery. Rocks are useful for building things or making a path.

After the run, it's time for breakfast. You are probably tired already but it's important to remember the rules and rituals of the meal. It is strictly vegetarian, you can't take a bite until the *Shifu* (master) starts eating, and you have to eat everything you put in your bowl. That won't be a problem because you're ravenous but you may balk at having to eat anything you drop on the floor. Stomach-churning this may be, but it does echo the Shaolin way: everything matters and nothing is wasted. God really is in the details.

After helping with the washing up, your kung fu session begins. Stretching exercises and gymnastic routines lead into an imaginary battle against multiple opponents. Lunch follows the first training session. You can then enjoy a short rest or teach a little English to anyone willing to learn. Your afternoon is filled with a 2-hour training session similar to the morning one.

Your evening downtime is spent with your fellow novices sitting round a fire in one of the monastery's dormitories. You'll tumble into bed exhausted at 8.30pm to sleep like a tree and get up again at five ready to do it all again.

Here, time is glacial. A week of this itinerary will feel like a month. But you may not want it to end. And if that's the case, your journey is really only just beginning.

EVERYDAY MONASTICISM

You don't have to go to a Shaolin temple or Christian monastery to live the monastic life. You can take the first steps now, today, in your bedroom. Are you ready for what your new life demands of you?

– Almost all monastic orders demand celibacy. This is a good early bellwether. If you can't handle the idea of never being physically intimate with anyone again then you aren't realistically going to be able to handle the trials of self-denial that lie ahead.

– Sell your Xbox. And your car, phone, TV, jewellery, and almost all your clothes. You have to let go of your worldly possessions. Monks across all religious orders leave their material goods behind. Sometimes, they sell the things they have and donate the proceeds to the church or temple.

– Meditate – or pray – for several hours a day. Buddhist, Christian and other monastic practices all emphasise focussing on achieving mental clarity and emotional calmness.

On most adventures it's the world that throws things in your way – extreme cold, thirst, wild animals, pain. But when you choose to live a monastic life you are subjecting yourself to trials and hardships. Why would you deny yourself worldly pleasures in such a way? What is to be gained from a life of asceticism? Those who have done it say that the reward is ultimate freedom.

Chongsheng Monastery, Dali

ONE MAN WHO MADE THE JOURNEY

When London-born Matthew Ahmet was 11, he was stunned by the theatre show *The Shaolin Wheel of Life*. It crystalized his growing love of martial arts and eastern culture and made him determined to visit the Shaolin Temple in China. For many of us that dream would fade with the passing of teenage years. For Matthew it only sharpened in focus. And when he was 16, he left home for China to begin Shaolin training. The regime was as intense as he imagined it would be: rising at 5.30am to run up a mountain, then crawling back down on his hands and knees, doing headstands on solid concrete for hours at a time. But Matthew's dedication paid off. Ten years after his epiphany in the theatre, he became the first and only non-Chinese Shaolin warrior invited to be a performer in that same show. His signature feat of strength is doing a handstand using only one finger on each hand.

COULD YOU KEEP UP WITH THE MARATHON MONKS?

No one goes quite as far in their search for enlightenment as the Tendai monks of Japan. Their philosophy holds that you can only reach that pure state through extreme self-denial. To prove this, they perform the 'Kaihogyo', a 1,000-day running challenge spread over seven years:

Year 1: run 18 miles a day for 100 straight days.

Year 2: same as Year 1.

Year 3: same again.

Year 4: same distance as before, but now for 200 days in a row.

Year 5: as Year 4.

Year 6: things have been a bit easy so far, so let's double the distance – you must run 36 miles per day for 100 days.

Year 7: you're in good nick now, so how about 52 miles for 100 days? (A double marathon every day!) After that you can wind down with a leisurely 18 miles on each of the final 100 days.

Even if you complete the running, your trials are not over. Rather than head swiftly to your nearest burger joint to eat the entire menu, you now have to enter a darkened room and spend nine days without food, water or sleep. The goal here is to utterly exhaust body and mind so you are as close as possible to death. Why? If you become enough of a void then the singularity of your spirituality will pop into existence and fill your emptiness with total understanding. It had better be worth it.

WHAT IS THE POINT?

What is the point of any adventure? There will always be downsides: pain, loneliness, fear, loss of hope. You will miss your family and friends, of course but also the smaller things that we take for granted every day, like hot running water, electricity, a soft bed.

But the simplicity of the monastic life fills your heart and sharpens your senses. As the weeks and months and years go by, your needs and desires will change. Less will please you more. The effort you put in to looking after your body, mind and soul will pay off. It will cost you a lot to reach a truly enlightened state, but yours will be a rich life indeed.

HEAVENLY PURSUITS

FÊTE DU VODOUN, BENIN

Priests offer blood-soaked animal sacrifices; young adherents cut themselves with knives as an act of devotion to their spirit protectors; groups of women dance themselves to a frenzy in front of a monument called the 'Gate of No Return'. This is the Fête du Vodoun, which every January attracts thousands of people a year to the coastal city of Ouidah to celebrate the much-misunderstood voodoo faith. The festivities last a full day and there's no strictly followed programme. Instead the day is an opportunity for disparate sects from across west Africa to join together.

The locally produced gin plays an active part in proceedings, not least when people try to achieve a trance-like state through highly exuberant dancing to a persistent drumbeat. You can tell who's managed to make it because they have their faces plastered in a white, talcum-like powder. The festival invariably ends on Ouidah's beach, where the music and dancing lasts long into the night.

Some people say the Fête du Vodoun is a slightly anaesthetized version of traditional tribal voodoo ceremonies but that's perhaps missing the point. A strict Marxist government in Benin prevented any public practising of voodoo for many years. When the regime changed in the early 1990s, the Festival was established to help the country reclaim its traditional culture and heritage. It's not just a religious observance, it's a celebration of being allowed to celebrate.

SEMANA SANTA, GUATEMALA

Easter in Guatemala is something special. The cobbled streets of the colonial city of Antigua host a succession of parades during Semana Santa (Holy Week) culminating in a day of processions on Good Friday which start well before dawn and go on deep into the night. The routes are carpeted with intricate 'alfombras'; richly coloured works of religious art, made out of dyed sawdust and augmented with flowers, which last only for a few hours before they're trampled by a procession of worshippers. The heady combination of colours, music and incense can be a lot to take in, as can negotiating the throbbing crowds, but you don't have to be a devout Christian to be moved by the strength of feeling.

TRAPPIST BEERS, BELGIUM

Where in the world can you combine religious observance with sinking a few amber nectars? Belgium, that's where. Brewing beer is a serious business in this part of the world, so much so that at six Trappist monasteries dotted around the country, communities of monks produce their own. Of this half-dozen, not all make their beer available to visitors but at Orval Abbey you can stay at a guesthouse and participate in monastic life. If you simply want to sample the goods, you can sip a beer at a café inside the abbey at Achel and watch while the monks go about their valuable work.

Voodoo festival, Ouidah, Benin

A KITE IN THE WIND
Paragliding

You climb into the back of the truck with the other newbies. The money is paid and the waiver is signed. It'll be harder to pull out now. With sweaty palms you sit in silence as the vehicle weaves its way up the mountain. It takes forever to drive up a series of switch backs to the launch site. Do you really need this level of excitement in your life?

By the time you reach the top you are formulating elaborate excuses to escape this insanity. The equipment is offloaded; a bag filled with nylon ropes connected to a wafer-thin 'chute, a tandem harness and some metal clips. You remind yourself that deaths relating to equipment failure are incredibly rare and that the drive up was probably more dangerous. Still, the thought of free-falling for 10 seconds before slamming into the deck if it all goes belly-up is rather hard to shake.

Spectators, armed with camera phones, are milling about the launch site and you are now committed to seeing this through. Time to focus and listen to your instructor. The canopy is laid out across the hillside and the ropes are untangled. Now strapped in and with pre-flight checks complete, it's time to run off a mountain.

Tandem flight,
Bourg d'Oisans, France

Your job is simple: keep running until your feet stop touching the ground. On the valley floor in the distance, you can see the landing zone – it looks so small.

You start to run and think you're airborne so you lift your legs. Too early, you land with a thud and tumble over as the canopy envelopes both of you.

"I didn't tell you to stop running!" yells your irritated instructor, his pride clearly dented. Back you go to try again. This time, just like Wile E. Coyote running off a cliff in the cartoon, your legs are still going ten-to-the-dozen five seconds after take-off.

But you are flying. When you look at your feet they dangle high above the valley floor like puppet legs on string.

At first, the ride is smoother than anticipated but you're not here to float down gently. After a few minutes you are 1,000 feet above the launch site and the whole of the Alps is laid out before you. Mont Blanc towers above and the Matterhorn shimmers in the distance. It feels like you're free as a bird. Quite simply, it's breathtaking.

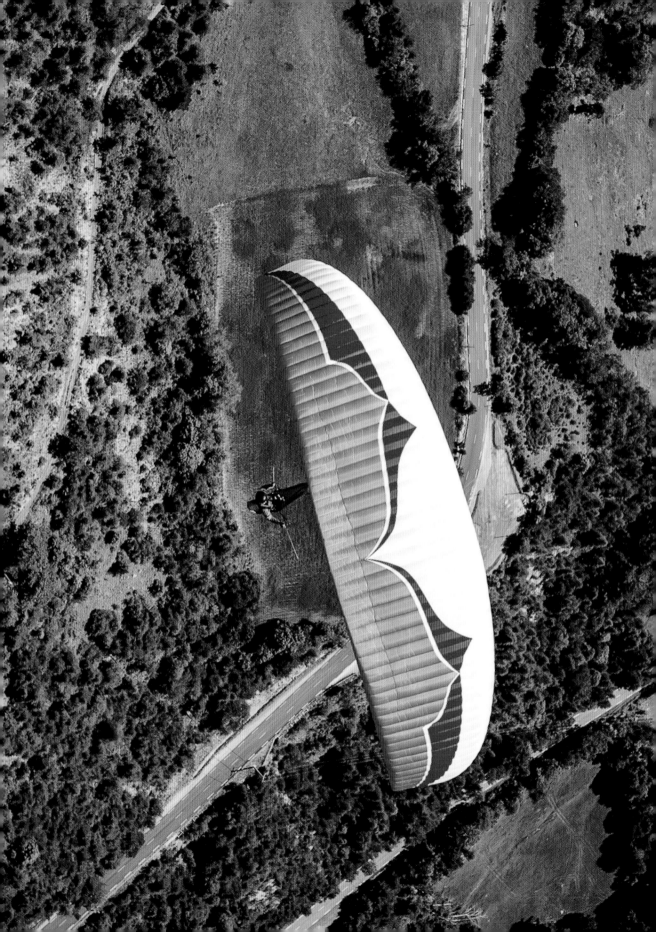

LAKE ANNECY, HAUTE-SAVOIE, FRANCE

TO GET YOUR CLUB PILOT LICENCE

DIFFICULTY   ★★★★☆

ENDURANCE   ★★★★★

NERVES OF STEEL ★★★★★

DURATION: 2 WEEKS MINIMUM
PERSONNEL: ONE, PLUS INSTRUCTOR
SKILLSET: HEAD FOR HEIGHTS (OBVIOUSLY),
             KNOWLEDGE OF AVIATION RULES
             AND REGULATIONS, MENTAL STRENGTH,
             HIGH FITNESS LEVEL
RISKS: UNPREDICTABLE WEATHER, EQUIPMENT FAILURE (LOW RISK),
             EXCEEDING YOUR LIMITS, GRAVITY!

Flying: 'moving or ability to move through the air with wings'.
Providing you are fit enough, paragliding is a sport you can start at just
about any age. Be warned though, it's highly addictive and many pilots
chase the feeling they had on their first flight for the rest of their life.

It's one thing to paraglide in tandem but nothing comes close to taking control of the reins yourself. And there are few better places in the world to learn than where it all started – the French Alps. Around Lake Annecy in particular, the scenery is spectacular and the local weather and wind patterns create superb conditions.

Paragliding (or *parapenting* as the French call it) began in Haute-Savoie when climbers in the 1960s started using small ram-air canopies to descend after their climbs. Before long it became apparent that, by using pockets of warm air (or 'thermals' – see panel on page 194), flight-times could be greatly extended. As technology advanced through the 80s and 90s, wingspans were increased, nonporous fabrics used and modifications were made to the shape and trim of the airfoil. New skills were required to fly and the sport became firmly established.

Around Lake Annecy and across the region there are lots of paragliding schools to choose from. Week-long beginner courses are a perfect introduction to the sport. Initially, you'll do tandem flights with an instructor, with the aim of completing your first short solo flight before the week is out. You'll be taught the mechanics of the wing, how it flies, what the wind does, how to steer and all the basics. Solo flight training starts with very short journeys of a few seconds on a gentle slope as you slowly build your skills and confidence. Advanced courses are also widely available so that you can progress and obtain your pilot licence.

MINDSETS; RIGHT & WRONG

There's an easy way to check if this activity is for you. When you see a bird soaring above, gliding effortlessly over the landscape, do you try to imagine what it must be like to be able to fly

A MIRACULOUS ESCAPE...
but don't let it put you off

The highest paraglide flight ever recorded was achieved by accident. German pilot Ewa Wisnierska was competing in a cross country competition in 2007. An enormous thunder cloud developed after the competition started. The storm acted like a giant vacuum cleaner and sucked in some of the competitors, including Ewa. Battling gale-force winds, heavy rain, giant hailstones and lightning, there was nothing they could do to stop themselves from being drawn upwards into the centre of the storm. At one point Eva was ascending at a rate of around 60 miles per hour.

By the time she reached 20,000 feet – well into the 'death zone' – she had passed out due to lack of oxygen and almost froze to death as temperatures dropped to -50°F. Above the storm now, she floated around at the edge of the stratosphere for 45 minutes while her body began to shut down. Suddenly, her wing collapsed and Eva plummeted to Earth. Just when all seemed lost, the wing incredibly popped open again and Ewa regained consciousness. The ordeal wasn't over though. Her core body temperature was life-threateningly low. Worse still, there was still a danger she could be sucked back into the storm. Amazingly, Ewa managed to steer herself away from danger and land. On the ground, a rescue party raced to the landing scene to save her before hypothermia took hold. It was a miraculous escape.

Ewa's GPS track-log recorded a height of 33,000 feet – 4,000 feet higher than Everest. All the other competitors managed to escape the storm with the exception of Chinese competitor He Zhongpin who, tragically, was less fortunate. Shaken but undeterred, a week later, Ewa flew again, in the same glider.

and wish you could? If the answer is 'no', you'd best find a different sport. If the answer is 'hell yes' then welcome aboard!

Too many people get into flying for the wrong reasons. Whether it's a mid-life crisis or some kind of replacement for something that seems to be absent from their lives, both are recipes for disaster. Every year stories emerge of people buying second-hand equipment online and trying their luck without proper training. The results are predictable. Do it because you want to learn to fly, and do it properly. It's essential to find an instructor who's right for you. Try to find someone you click with; so talk to a few and get a feel for what they are like.

Paragliding isn't as dangerous as you might think, providing certain rules are followed:

* Work out what your limits are and operate well within them. Risk aversion is always best.

* When your gut tells you the conditions aren't safe, don't be a lemming and follow others off the cliff. Don't ignore bad weather.

* No matter how experienced you become, never get complacent when it comes to pre-flight checks and planning.

It helps to have a keen interest in aviation. If you apply the same basic safety rules that commercial airline pilots employ, you'll stand a much better chance of staying safe. As your experience builds you'll know more about the weather than the forecasters on TV, and weather watching will take over your life.

You must be honest with yourself. Recognize that you are scared, you should and need to be. Blanking out your senses will inevitably lead to poor decision-making and you need your wits about you all the time. Few sports are as

* Paragliding is not to be confused with hang gliding. Both are unpowered but a hang glider has a rigid aluminium frame covered by fabric.

* In the Alps, pilots generally reach heights of 11,500 feet. If conditions are perfect around Mt Blanc, heights of 16,000 feet are achievable.

* Cross country competitions are all about distance. Whoever gets the furthest, in any direction, wins.

* The longest straight-line distance covered is 344 miles, set by three Brazilian pilots who flew for 11 hours in 2016.

* Although it's a male-dominated sport, in the French Alps around one-third of paragliders are women with more coming into the sport each year.

mentally absorbing but that's also part of the attraction.

Once you start flying solo, continue to practice your ground skills over and over. Some instructors recommend novices complete 100 take-offs and landings before they start hunting down thermals. But, once you know what you are doing, the beautiful thing about paragliding is that you don't need anyone else. Grab your pack, up you go and fly, completely free. When you catch a thermal for the first time and climb higher and higher, you won't want to be anywhere else *on* Earth.

HOW DO THERMALS WORK?

Thermals are currents of air that have a huge effect on paragliding. When sunlight hits the ground it warms it up. The heat from the ground then warms the air above and a thermal 'bubble' may be released. Crucially, what's on the ground can determine how strong the thermal will be. Darker ground coverage, like a ploughed field or an asphalt car park, will absorb more energy from the sun so thermals are stronger there.

The best flying conditions are often found immediately after a weather front passes through. The air above is cooler, so warm air below can rise to high elevations.

Significantly, for paragliding, excellent thermals are also generated on exposed mountain ridges, especially earlier in the day. As the sun comes up its rays hit these ledges directly, so they warm quickly. When conditions are good, and the pilot continues to find thermals, it's possible to stay up in the air for many hours and, by using the prevailing wind, cover huge distances.

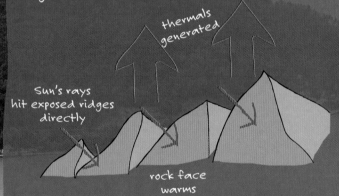

thermals generated

Sun's rays hit exposed ridges directly

rock face warms

Conversely, if there is a lot of moisture on the ground or in the air, most of the sun's energy is used up in the evaporation process so thermals are weak. If you see a paraglider above a lake, they are almost certainly descending through cooler, sinking air. Similarly, in winter when snow covers the ground, thermals are weak. Staying airborne is much more difficult.

Lake Annecy

SOAR AROUND THE GLOBE

You can go paragliding just about anywhere in the world – that's one of the main attractions. But while you are learning you must find somewhere with generally stable weather conditions and where there are lots of schools to choose from. Novices should start on easy, gentle, obstacle-free take-off zones above large, flat landing sites away from pylons, buildings and busy roads.

ANDALUCIA, SPAIN

Southern Spain has one of the warmest climates in Europe and the sun shines over 90 percent of the time. It also has reliable winds and terrific thermals. So, while the rest of Europe is still gripped by winter, paragliders can take advantage of superb year-round conditions. You can fly from the mountains to the sea and on clear days the views across to Morocco in North Africa are fabulous.

RAYONG, THAILAND

Proximity to the Gulf of Thailand helps create consistent winds that provide excellent conditions to master ground handling skills. The training hills are gentle and free of obstructions, perfect for confidence-building on those nerve-racking first solo flights. With Bangkok just a two-hour drive away, getting there is easy.

ROLDANILLO, COLOMBIA

Los Tanques is the main take-off site some 3,000 feet above the town of Roldanillo. From the top, the wide Cauca Valley and unfenced farmland stretch out beneath you to the east. Influenced by the Trade Winds, the humid, tropical weather conditions usually guarantee stable thermals across a wide area. With mountains to the west acting as a barrier, winds are normally light and thermals fairly gentle. A word of caution though – during dry periods conditions can become more difficult, especially for inexperienced pilots.

Lhotse, Nepal

After a few lessons you'll be
ready for the Himalayas!
Okay, not really, but once
you're an expert this is
where you could be flying.

"Being able to survive in the wilderness isn't a macho, physical thing. To have any chance of succeeding you must win your own psychological battles first."

MAKE TRACKS
Mountain biking

Approaching climb eight of nine you prepare your mind and body for more torture. Your face is caked in mud and dried sweat. There's a metallic taste in your mouth from the previous climb. That metal taste is blood – the extreme exertion has inflamed the lining of your throat and nose.

Some riders have given up before the climb even starts – no judgment though. You keep your speed up for the first minute or two but gravity takes its toll. Your thigh muscles burn as acid conquers parts of your body that oxygen currently can't reach.

It takes all your effort to keep things going. The bike is barely moving and remains upright only because you weave back and forth across the narrow track. Your thighs are an inferno now.

Your only thoughts are of reaching the top, nothing else on Earth matters.

Just when you think your lungs are about to explode, finally, wondrously, the terrain starts to level off. You've made it and within a few seconds you're freewheeling. The joy of the descent is indescribable. One more climb to go – you're starting to believe you can make it.

CAPE EPIC, WESTERN CAPE, SOUTH AFRICA
The bike burial ground

In 2004, experienced mountain biker Kevin Vermaak's vision to create the toughest event of its kind came to fruition. It set a benchmark for the sport and helped to spark a mountain biking revolution in South Africa. Put simply, it's brutal.

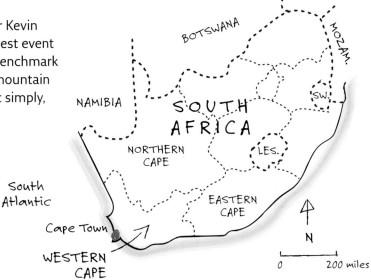

DIFFICULTY **★★★★**★

ENDURANCE **★★★★**★

NERVES OF STEEL **★★**★★★

DURATION:	8 DAYS (MARCH/APRIL)
PERSONNEL:	TEAMS OF TWO
SKILLSET:	SEASONED MOUNTAIN BIKER
RISKS:	EXTREME FATIGUE, DEHYDRATION, COLLISIONS & CRASHES AT HIGH SPEED ON STEEP, ROCKY TERRAIN, KIDNEY-RELATED ILLNESSES

Billed as the mountain biking equivalent of the Tour de France, this eight-day, 500-mile race in the South African heat is unrivalled in its rawness. Now owned by the Ironman brand, the Cape Epic is the most televised mountain bike stage race in the world. But it's not just for pro riders; amateurs can follow in the dust of those seeking podium spots and international fame.

It's the only eight-day mountain bike race unclassified by the Union Cycliste Internationale (UCI) – it's so difficult they ran out of categories. Only four other international UCI events in the world carry the SHC (Stage Hors Categorie status): Vuelta a España, Giro d'Italia, Cyprus' Sunshine Cup and the Tour de France.

THE SETTING

Almost immediately after its inception, the Cape Epic quickly became infamous in the biking community for its sheer hellishness. For a start, over the course of eight days, there is on average 50,000 ft of climbing – more than three whole Mont Blancs' worth. The route changes annually but it takes two years for the route team to research, test and map the toughest terrain they can find in the untamed Western Cape.

The terrain is harsh, with dusty gravel tracks, heart-bursting craggy ascents, terrifying technical descents, narrow forested ridges, rickety bridges and challenging mud and river traverses. Temperatures vary enormously from bitterly cold, frosty mornings to unrelenting heat in the afternoons. It's not uncommon for temperatures to top 104°F (40°C).

The organizers' careful planning ensures the riders – and TV cameras following the pro race – get to see all that the Western Cape has to offer, including spectacular rocky outcrops, steep ravines, native woodlands, weather-beaten coastlines, remote villages and picture-perfect vineyards. Climbs are meticulously planned to push riders to their absolute limits. This is a proper test of mental and physical preparation.

THE RACE

Securing a spot is difficult, as it's over-subscribed each year. There is an early bird entry system but you need to be very quick since those places are usually sold out within minutes. There is also a lottery system, or you can enter via one of the event's charities but that comes at a premium. A better way perhaps is to join the volunteer programme. You'll get an insider's perspective of what the event entails and guaranteed entry the following year.

There are 650 teams of two so you need to find a racing partner if you are fortunate enough to get in. Best choose your buddy wisely because if they fail, you do too. Competitors who lose their partners are allowed to continue solo. They must not interfere in any way with the race, and have to wear a white 'Outcast' jersey.

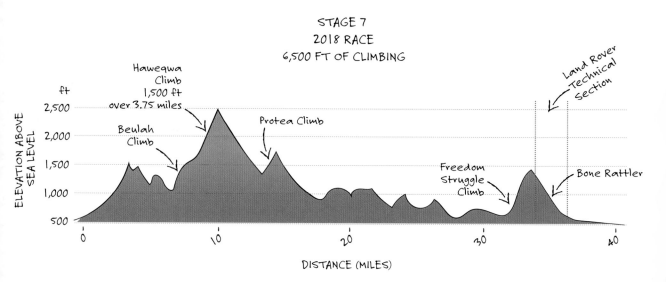

STAGE 7
2018 RACE
6,500 FT OF CLIMBING

Czech rider
Jaroslav Kulhavy,
2018 race

MAKE UP YOUR OWN ADVENTURE: BIKEPACKING

A mix of wild camping and biking, taking all your kit with you so you can eat and sleep en route allows you to venture deep into the wilderness for several days or more. If you are going away for a very long trip and refuelling as you go, sourcing cheap and readily available spare parts is essential. It's sensible to keep things simple and taking a bike with full suspension and lots of components that can go wrong is asking for trouble.

You should be pretty decent at general bike maintenance. Although in the workshop it's easier to replace a punctured inner tube with a new one, you'll need to go old-school and reacquaint yourself with a puncture repair kit ahead of this excursion. It will boost your confidence if you can deal with most mechanical emergencies on your own.

Good planning minimizes the risk of things going wrong on your adventure. It also helps you work out exactly what equipment you need and what you can live without. If you are new to it and planning a multi-day trip, best do a trial overnighter and you'll quickly figure out what you do and, more likely, don't need. The main tip: less is more.

Partners must remain within two minutes of each other throughout the race or face a one-hour penalty with a three-strikes-and-you're-out rule. Often held on Table Mountain, the event starts with the Prologue, followed by seven even more gruelling stages. Within each category, winning is simple: you just need to be the team with the lowest time overall.

"At some point on the speedbumps on the Land Rover technical section, my back wheel overtook my front wheel and sent me over the bar and I landed face-first in the muck. Knocked myself out.

I was quite lucky I suppose, no broken bones in the face, a few broken ribs, no damage to the eye itself, couple of scars and some plastic surgery. Should be back on the bike soon."

(South African rugby legend Joel Stransky's account of his crash in the 2017 Prologue. He also punctured a lung during the crash!)

The pro race is essentially separate. Eighty percent of competitors are amateurs so there's no need to worry that you'll be the lone riders receiving sympathy cheers from spectators while the advertising hoardings are packed up. However, you must finish each stage within the specified maximum time or you're out.

The professional riders have their support teams with them which may seem unfair. What about the rest of us? Well, here's the good news: the Cape Epic is fully serviced, which means 'all' you have to do is focus on riding, as the race organizers take care of everything else. That's right: food, tented accommodation and even mechanical assistance – result!

Before you get too excited, this doesn't make the race any easier, it just means almost all your prep time in the months before can be spent on training and not logistics. Just as well.

It's quite a thrill to be in a race with some of your professional heroes with the TV helicopters buzzing overhead. Okay, you might not get very close to them but the spectators who wave them off and cheer en route will do the same for you.

PREPARATION

For such an extreme event, diet plays a critical role, not only during the competition but also through the months of training, as explained by nutritionist and sport scientist Adrian Pezhorn: "You need to trial your nutritional strategy before the event and work out what's best for you. It's too late at the event to start eating different gels; take into the race what you've trained with."

The amount of climbing is not to be underestimated and the organizers don't shy away from telling you. Your legs and lungs better be ready or you'll not last a day. You'll need to push

Chain trouble on the course

WHY ARE PRO BIKES SO EXPENSIVE?

Top-end bikes can cost a king's ransom. Those not in the know wonder why a fairly simple-looking mode of transport can be more expensive than a car. What makes mountain bikes so ridiculously pricey?

The truth is that, really, they're not.

If you're looking in a shop window at a bike with a price tag nudging towards five figures, you are eyeing up one of the very best racing machines that this sport has to offer. The clue is in the name – it's a 'pro' bike.

It's all relative. Buying a perfectly serviceable mid-range mountain bike doesn't have to break the bank and it will still do a very good job.

At a professional level, weight, strength and efficiency are everything. So, a pro bike will have a lightweight carbon fibre frame, electronic gear shifting, disc brakes and hand-built wheels. Take almost every component on a standard bike and the pro bikes will have replaced them with something much lighter and tighter. Even the ball bearings on the wheels will be made of ceramic instead of steel. It all adds up.

The law of diminishing marginal returns kicks in as the price tag rises. But, when the difference between success and failure can be a few seconds, what's another two grand for the very best drivechain, gear shifters and brakes!

After five minutes on the Cape Epic, this would be reduced to firewood!

yourself to the limit and beyond on training climbs in the months before. So, whatever prep you normally do for a race, double that and then some.

Much like a peloton on road races, competitors often bunch up to ride in each other's slipstream. It's one thing to ride wheel to wheel on smooth tarmac, but on a bumpy track at speed a very cool head is required. Get comfortable doing this during training.

Your bike will take an absolute beating and it won't be uncommon for it to need major surgery every day – luckily, you'll have bike mechanics on hand to help. You don't need to be a genius to work out that you need a good quality bike to cope with the relentlessly tough terrain. It'll need 29-inch wheels preferably, dual-suspension, single or double chain ring (not triple) and a carbon frame. These features will help you cope on the bumps and dips.

However, it's not worth agonizing over which one to choose, or to spend a fortune. Make sure the bike you have is well maintained and it'll do just fine. Let's be clear, fitness and endurance are far more critical factors. It may sound obvious but make sure you train on the bike you plan to use and position the brake levers, gear shifters and bars just as you want them so your bike feels comfortable from the off.

The contact points on the bike – the grips, saddle and pedals – are important, so choose wisely. You'll need a saddle on which you'll be comfortable for 10 hours and that allows you to sit down at the end of the day without requiring an ice pack for your butt. Thorns are a constant nuisance so make sure whatever tyres you use have some form of protection and reinforced tread to cope. If you don't, they'll be ripped to shreds and that'll be the end of your race.

No shame in walking on the toughest climbs

During the competition, you'll need to carry your bike over the most difficult terrain. Don't be ashamed to do this if it means you can preserve precious energy and still make it up in the same time.

Other mountain bike events will put forward compelling arguments to suggest their race is tougher. Some will decry the commercialism now associated with the race. Ignore the critics because the Cape Epic continues to set the standard for extreme mountain biking the world over. And, significantly, its popularity among the elite and serious amateurs alike shows no sign of abating.

If you manage to get in – and better still, finish – you can dine out on your achievement forever more.

OR TRY THESE RACES

TRANS ALP, AUSTRIA, GERMANY & ITALY (JULY)

Mountain biking and the Alps are a match made in heaven. Most of the big ski resorts now open their lifts during the summer providing access to hundreds of miles of varied mountain terrain. Some, such as the Portes du Soleil ski region straddling France and Switzerland, have so many linked lifts that you can cover huge distances in a single day. Plus, it's pretty cool to pop over to another country within the same ride.

There are lots of organized races in the Alps but one in particular stands out. Now in its 21st year, the TransAlp race belongs to a small group of trailblazing competitions. It's part-race, part-expedition as the riders have to cross the eastern Alps on a route that varies slightly each year. The 2018 race went from Imst in the Tirol region of Austria to Arco in Italy, with the 2019 event going in the opposite direction. Rules are similar to the Cape Epic with two riders per team and 600 teams per year.

YAK ATTACK, ANNAPURNA RANGE, NEPAL (NOVEMBER)

The Yak Attack is the highest long-distance mountain bike race in the world – it reaches the oxygen-depleted altitude of 18,000 feet above sea level. To finish, you'll need to cope with the following: extreme temperature variations (we're talking highs of 85°F and lows of 5°F), sand, dust, mud, snow, ice and biting winds. Plus, there are rickety suspension bridges, horrendously steep single tracks and, of course, wandering Yaks to contend with.

You'll have to carry your bike across snowfields while you gasp for breath and ignore precipitous drops. The week-long event is a bit more rough and ready than most other races with just dozens rather than hundreds of entrants. But this simply adds to its appeal and it's not as expensive to enter as you might think. The rewards? How many people get to say they've ridden across the roof of the world?

Muktinath, Nepal, Yak Attack

Although the mountains here are lower than further west, the climbs are demanding and the views stunning. Riders cross one or more mountain passes on each stage during the brief period in the year when they are snow-free. It's aimed at amateurs but it lasts for seven days, covering 315 miles, with 60,000 feet of climbing – it's no Sunday afternoon park ride. Add in the mix of cultures as you ride from one region to another and the result is mountain biking perfection.

CROCODILE TROPHY, NORTHERN QUEENSLAND, AUSTRALIA (OCTOBER)

The oldest and still one of the most gruelling mountain bike stage races in the world takes place in North Queensland each spring. Around 120 solo cyclists compete on a route that takes them through lush tropical rainforest and Aussie Outback. Recreational cyclists can participate in the final three stages to get a taste of what it's like to do the whole eight-day race.

WILD SWIMMING

Open water swims

Dive into the sea from one continent, swim awhile, get out the water in a different continent. Why do it? Because why the hell not, that's why. An intercontinental swim is well within reach of anyone who's willing to train and knows their way around a front crawl. The real question is, where? There's a surprisingly healthy number of options to choose from, ranging from a short, sharp dip in sub-Arctic waters to, well, a long, gruelling slog through sub-Arctic waters.

In between there's a myriad of possibilities at pinch points across the globe. It's possible to enter events which will see you travel together with hundreds of fellow athletes, or to arrange a solo crossing with the support of groups that have been specifically set up to help with these challenges.

However you choose to do it, you'll have to get used to the subtle art of open water swimming, of tailoring your technique to accommodate swells and currents, and preparing your body to withstand exposure to the elements.

THE STRAIT OF GIBRALTAR

Swim from Europe to Africa across the Strait of Gibraltar. You'll be negotiating a narrow pass where the Mediterranean Sea meets the Atlantic Ocean on a journey that can measure anything from 8-12 miles, depending on the strength and direction of currents.

DIFFICULTY **★★★**★★

ENDURANCE **★★★★**★

NERVES OF STEEL **★★★**★★

DURATION: 3–6 HOURS
PERSONNEL: YOU, PLUS A SUPPORT CREW
SKILLSET: OPEN WATER SWIMMING: STAMINA, NAVIGATION
RISKS: SEA CURRENTS, HYPOTHERMIA, SUNSTROKE, BIG SHIPS (AND SMALL ONES)

The distinctive Rock of Gibraltar has overseen traffic in and out of the Mediterranean Sea for as long as humans have been using boats to travel the world. This huge lump of limestone, a British overseas territory on the southern tip of Spain, juts 1,400 ft up from the shore and into the clouds. From the top, Morocco and the African coastline seem tantalizingly close – not much more than a quick dip when the sky is blue and the sea is calm. At sea level, however, you realize that actually getting from one side to the other under your own steam is going to be a bit of an effort.

For one thing, the wind can whip up to dangerous speeds while you're out on the water. For another, the Strait is one of the world's busiest shipping lanes, with supertankers and gargantuan cruise ships squeezing through this narrow pass on the way to and from the Suez Canal.

There's good news too, though. The prevailing currents surge from west to east, which means you'll be naturally guided towards your target destination and not tugged out into the vast expanse of the Atlantic. The even better news is that you'll have a helping hand to organize your

OPEN WATER SWIMMING TECHNIQUES

BEFORE YOU HEAD OUT

Learn to breathe on both sides of your stroke – it makes it easier to swim in a straight line. In a swimming pool there are lines on the bottom to keep you straight. Open water doesn't have lines. Waves can obscure your view of the shore; so can foggy goggles and sunlight reflecting off the water. Regulate your technique to stay on a straight and narrow path. You also need to be able to look forward regularly to check you are on course. Practise using your forward momentum to 'pop up' just before you breathe.

Open water is colder than pools. Swimming with a quicker stroke rate helps you keep warm. The world's best open water swimmers make 70-100 strokes per minute. This can take time to learn because your body simply isn't used to powering your arms at such an aerobic rate.

crossing attempt. The Gibraltar Strait Swimming Association (known as ACNEG) processes all applications to swim the Strait. There are a few hoops to jump through if you want to give it a go. You'll have to give them medical records, a resumé of your open water swimming credentials and a couple of thousand euros if you want to make it on to their departure list. In return, they'll arrange official permissions for your adventure, provide two boats and crew to accompany you on the way and a medical support team, just in case. If you complete the swim, you even get a certificate to frame.

RACING THE CURRENT

Crossing attempts start from the Spanish town of Tarifa, a nice, quiet place that unfortunately suffers from a bit of a wind problem. This part of the coast is given a good buffeting by gusts blowing in from the middle of the Mediterranean and sometimes the wait for calm conditions can take a while. As in several days. It's pretty frustrating to sit on the beach watching windsurfers having a whale of a time when all you want is for their sails to go still. This is why you'll be given a window of several days during which your crossing attempt will take place, rather than a specific date.

When the organizers are happy that you won't be blown off course, you'll be escorted down to a clump of rocks near the shore and told to wait for the sound of the starter's pistol, which will serve as your launch signal.

About 60 swimmers a year tackle the crossing and the success rate is pretty good, but there's one absolutely key factor in making it to Morocco – a fast start.

TAKING THE PLUNGE

Research your swim site. Examine the tides, current, wildlife and other water users. Do you have an escape plan if you are out there alone and get tired halfway? Note landmarks that will be visible from the water: islands, trees, cliffs and buildings, for instance. The sun can be the easiest navigation aid of all.

KEEP AT IT

Your first few swims may seem to last forever, with very little distance covered. Don't worry. Elite open water swimmers often train for a set time rather than distance. Your first few outings may not be that enjoyable, but your comfort in open water really will increase with experience. Finally, you will have negative thoughts as it's just you and the water with few distractions. Try yelling those thoughts out loud. Screaming, "This water's bloody FREEZING!" or "I hate waves!" gets the thoughts out of your system and stops them replaying on a loop in your brain when you don't want them to.

SPAIN

MOROCCO

The point-to-point distance from Tarifa to your African landing point is just over nine miles but the tides and currents are your friends here. They'll sweep you along in an easterly direction, towards your destination, which means that each stroke will have a little bit of natural assistance behind it, shortening your journey. But this only matters if you can swim fast enough to reach the helpful water in good time.

The currents that'll give you a boost don't come into play when you're near the coast. You need to get out to the deep for them to work their magic and, if you can't do that quickly enough, fatigue will set in and your chances will recede with the tide. ACNEG recommend an absolute minimum speed of two kilometres per hour to stand a realistic chance of making it and something closer to 3 kmph if you want to avoid spending too much time in water that can be perilously cold.

SHIP HAPPENS

Some open water swims are a wonderful way of communing with nature. This is not one of them.

For one thing there are ships, lots and lots of them, some of them so big that they wouldn't even notice munching over a swimmer or two as they sail along. AGNEG operate with the assistance of shipping traffic control in both Spain and Morocco to keep you clear of harm but, if there is a threat of a collision, your support crew will pull you out the water and clear the area, then return you to the spot once the danger has passed. Not ideal, perhaps, but infinitely better than locking horns with a multi-ton supertanker.

There might be plenty of ships, but there's not much marine life to keep you company. You might spot the occasional jellyfish idly floating about but this isn't the kind of place where friendly seals and dolphins cavort nearby for your viewing pleasure. The area round the Strait is home to a pod of orca – which may explain the absence of seals and dolphins – and it's not unknown for a crew member to spot a dorsal fin breaching the water's surface in the near distance. However, close encounters with these ocean giants are pretty much unheard of.

Most crossings take between four and five hours. If you're in the water for more than seven, you're likely to get a 'hurry up or get out' message from your support crew. There are some people who have crossed in a real hurry. Georgios Charcharis, from Greece, made it in two hours and nine minutes in 2009.

However long it takes, an unmistakable surge of adrenalin will flood your body as you home in on the endpoint of your adventure, at Punta Cires in Morocco. The rocky coastline here makes it difficult to get out the water but just a touch of the rocky shore is enough to confirm you've made it. Climb aboard your support vessel, treat yourself to a rewarding energy supplement (or maybe something stronger), sit back and relax. You are now part of a special gang – the trans-continental swimmers.

SEVENTH HEAVEN

What if swimming the Strait of Gibraltar gives you a taste for more of the same? Fortunately, there's a multi-continental challenge just waiting for you. The Ocean's Seven is a collection of epic crossings around the world, ranging in difficulty from extremely tough to absolutely bloody terrifying. The other six are:

THE COOK STRAIT, NEW ZEALAND

One in six swimmers who attempt this 16-mile crossing between New Zealand's North and South Islands report an encounter with a shark. Don't worry, though, nobody has been attacked – yet. Anyway, the immense tidal surges are a far more immediate threat to your chances.

THE KA'IWI CHANNEL, HAWAI'I, USA

This stretch of water between the islands of Molokai and Oahu is invitingly warm and flanked by stunning coastal scenery. It's also very bouncy. Progress through 26 miles of rolling swells and strong currents requires serious skill and fitness.

THE ENGLISH CHANNEL, UK/FRANCE

Arguably the most famous channel swim of them all measures 21 miles across a busy shipping route. The first successful attempt was in 1875 by Englishman Matthew Webb and took 21 hours. More than 2,000 swimmers have followed in Webb's wake.

THE CATALINA CHANNEL, CALIFORNIA, USA

This challenge starts in one of the world's biggest metropolises and finishes in the serene quietness of Santa Catalina Island. In between are 21 miles of deep-water swimming which can only realistically be tackled during a four-month weather window from June to September.

THE TSUGARU STRAIT, JAPAN

The sea between Honshu and its northern neighbour, Hokkaido, is battered by strong winds and fierce currents. The Strait is 12 miles as the crow flies but the established route is six miles longer. Watch out for oil tankers. And venomous sea snakes.

THE NORTH CHANNEL, UK

Regarded by many open water experts as the toughest of all, the 21-mile traverse from Northern Ireland to Scotland is a real handful. Strong currents and tides, body-breaking cold and lots of lion's mane jellyfish threaten your progress. Kim Chambers was stung more than 200 times during her 2014 crossing and needed hospital treatment for toxic shock.

Bosphorus Strait, 2014

MORE OPEN WATER SWIMS

TURKEY

Hundreds huddle on the eastern shore of the Bosphorus Strait, at a spot in the northern reaches of Istanbul, once every year to take part in the world's most popular trans-continental swim. It takes less than an hour for the fastest entrants to get from Kanlica in Asia to Kuruçeşme in Europe – the record time is an impressive 39 minutes. The Bosphorus Cross Continental Swim is the one day of the year when it's possible to make this four-mile journey. Anyone who tries to swim across without a lockdown on shipping transport is likely to come off second best in an argument with one of the thousands of seagoing vessels that use this stretch of water every day.

The swim is restricted to 1,200 non-Turkish participants each year so plan well ahead if you fancy giving it a crack – there's fierce competition for places.

ICELAND

If the idea of swimming between two continents interests you but the thought of being pitched into all that open water makes your head, erm... swim, then go to Thingvellir National Park in Iceland. Here you'll find the Silfra fissure where in the cold, clear water it's possible to snorkel between two continental plates in a matter of seconds. On one side you have North America, on the other, Europe.

WALK ON THE WILD SIDE

Safari by foot

Your guide jabs his fist in the air – a silent gesture commanding you to stay absolutely still. Your eyes scan the scrubland but nothing registers... why the sudden stop? Slowly, very slowly, your guide points towards an unmoving object about 50 yards away. And once you focus, you can't believe you missed it before; a solitary black rhino standing perfectly still except for an occasional snap of an ear to keep the flies away.

There's no noise to speak of; it's a scene of perfect tranquillity. Just you, your small posse of fellow travellers, one massive, grunting, snorting miracle of nature and your guide with his AK47.

You stare, transfixed, until quite suddenly and with a surprising lightness of hoof, the object of your attention turns tail and trots off into the bush.

It's an encounter you'll never forget and a very particular reminder that sometimes the old ways are still the best.

NORTH LUANGWA NATIONAL PARK, ZAMBIA

Slap-bang in the ancient heart of Africa sits a pocket of paradise where human beings are the interlopers and animals have the run of the place. The concept of walking safaris was more or less invented in North Luangwa National Park. It's still one of the best spots on Earth to experience this entirely different kind of animal adventure.

DIFFICULTY **★★★★★**
ENDURANCE **★★★★★**
NERVES OF STEEL **★★★★★**

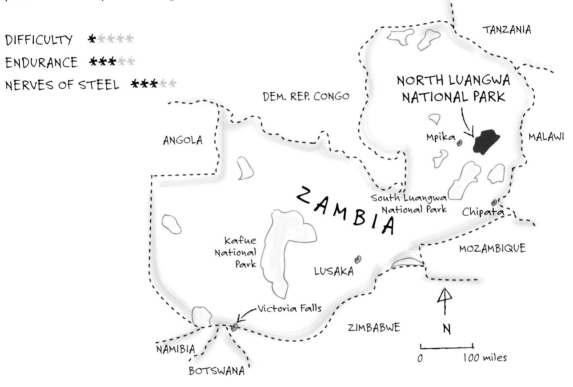

DURATION: 5–7 DAYS
PERSONNEL: TWO ARMED GUIDES, AND THREE OR FOUR WALKING COMPANIONS
SKILLSET: STEALTH, STAMINA
RISKS: YOU ARE NO LONGER AT THE TOP OF THE FOOD CHAIN

The North Luangwa National Park is tucked away in a quiet corner of Zambia. Getting there can be awkward. It doesn't have any roads to speak of, or villages, or hotels, or cafés, or anything like that. And as a result there's another thing the park doesn't have a lot of – tourists.

Only 500 visitors annually come to this patch of Africa. To put it in context, the Las Vegas Strip gets more visitors in 10 minutes than North Luangwa gets in a year.

So – other than the fact that it couldn't be more different from Las Vegas – what's the point of seeking it out? Well, what North Luangwa lacks in humans it more than makes up for in other, more interesting, species. It's home to lions, elephants, buffalo, an endemic species of zebra, leopards, hippos (lots and lots of hippos) and even a sprinkling of critically endangered black rhino. This pristine wilderness is part of Africa's Great Rift Valley, the starting point for all human existence. And the best way – the only way – to find out what it's got to offer is to turn your back on the 21st century and explore the place on foot.

North Luangwa National Park sprawls over 2,900 square miles along the banks of Luangwa River. It's far from the biggest national park in Africa but when you're only covering six or seven miles a day on foot, it's plenty big enough. Access to the park is strictly regulated. You'll need to sign up with one of the authorized travel companies for the duration of your visit but that's not really a problem; you're going to need expert guidance and someone with a gun to make sure you get the most from the trip anyway - and to make sure that you don't get eaten.

NO PASSENGERS

So why choose to walk your safari when there are perfectly good vehicles to transport you through the bush? It's all a question of perspective. Modern safaris and game drives are better-placed than ever before to put you in the path of as much wildlife as possible. Satellite imagery, drones and GPS tracking mean there aren't really any hiding places any more in the

Hotel!

Troop of baboons drinking from the Luangwa river

big game reserves. As a consequence of this, it's easier for more people to get to the animal hotspots. In some parks your close encounter with nature will be shared with a throng of off-road vehicles, packed with camera-wielding sightseers, circled round a slightly startled animal. It can all feel a bit clinical.

Taking to the savannah on foot, with a handful of fellow hikers, feeling the earth under your boots and immersing yourself in the wilderness is a dramatically different experience. You probably won't be able to tick as many animals off your 'seen it' list but you will get a feel for the wilderness that you won't enjoy from the back of

an SUV. You're not just a passenger on someone else's journey.

You'll have to attune your senses to the atmosphere of the bush and acknowledge your place in the grand scheme of things. A legacy of humankind's impact on nature is that many animals will turn tail and run rather than risk an encounter with *homo sapiens*. An expert guide will help you to understand the park's flora and fauna so that you gain an appreciation for the day-to-day movements of many fascinating species in a way that goes far beyond a mere photo opportunity.

GET YOUR GUIDE RIGHT

For independent-minded travellers who are used to striking their own path, a walking safari can be frustrating at times because there is a very definite chain of command, with your guide leaders calling the shots and you and your fellow walkers taking orders. It has to be that way – the wilderness is no place for a management strategy meeting.

RHINO CHARGES AND HOW TO SURVIVE THEM

Black rhinos aren't the biggest members of the family but they're certainly the nastiest. They're notorious for their charge-first-ask-questions-later approach to life. North Luangwa is home to only a few dozen of these foul-tempered beasts but, should you wander into one's path, here's how to make sure you don't end up hanging from its horn:

* Rhinos don't bluff. If one starts a charge it isn't going to change its mind.

* Rhinos are fast. A charging Black will cover 30 yards in three seconds. You probably can't match that, unless your name is Usain Bolt, so don't try to outsprint it.

* Case the joint. If you encounter a rhino, immediately take note of the options for cover around you – trees in particular.

* Bigger is better. A motivated rhino can easily flatten a small tree. You're looking for one that's at least a foot in diameter.

* Keep climbing. Makes sure you get above horn reach – try to climb as high as you can.

* Hit the deck. You definitely don't want to be standing in front of a charging rhino. If you can't reach a tree dive to the ground, facing the rhino feet first.

* Roll with it. You're on the ground and impact is imminent, roll to the side as quickly as you can.

* Good luck!

BACK TO NATURE

It's no coincidence that North Luangwa was one of the first African national parks to seize on the concept of walking safaris: its landscape is perfectly suited to the purpose. The park is situated between the Luangwa river to the west and the mighty Muchinga Escarpment which towers more than 3,000 ft high to the east. In between sits a gloriously varied range of habitats; from savannah dotted with distinctive sausage trees, to thickets of acacia bushes, to thick woodlands of mahogany and leadwood. There is no permanent visitor accommodation and only a few fixed camps. Most likely you'll be staying in a pop-up camp which feels somehow fitting given your surroundings and the nature of your visit.

The best time of year to go is in the dry season from June to October. Most walking tours explore the area along the Mwaleshi River, a tributary of the Luangwa, which dwindles to a trickle in the summer and forces wildlife to gather round the water pools that remain in the dry season heat.

It's impossible to predict with certainty the animals you'll see but there are some species that thrive in North Luangwa. The park's hippo population is one of the most robust in Africa, and elephant numbers – nearly destroyed by the atrocity of poaching in the 1970s and 80s – are growing all the time.

WHERE THE BUFFALO ROAM

If any encounter is almost guaranteed, it's one with a buffalo – North Luangwa is packed with them. And where there are buffalo, there are animals that eat buffalo. Prides of lions follow the herd on land while massive Nile crocodiles help themselves to any that enter their riverbank

domain. If you're lucky – really, really lucky – you might see a black rhino. If your luck runs out, it might see you. Black rhino are notoriously short-tempered. The fact you could see them at all is down to a ground-breaking reintroduction programme which, since 2003, has seen 34 of these moody, magnificent beasts brought back to one of their old stomping grounds.

But obsessing about which animals you'll see is missing the point. Of course it's great to witness a hunting pride of lions making a kill, or a pack of elephants ambling along, but the simple thrill of being in one of the world's last great wildernesses is what makes your walk so special. Over days, as you become more attuned to your surroundings, you'll find that talk with your fellow travellers becomes less frequent, your camera tends to stay in your pocket and the mechanics of modern travelling are stripped away.

What's left is an adventure that's thrillingly, uniquely pure.

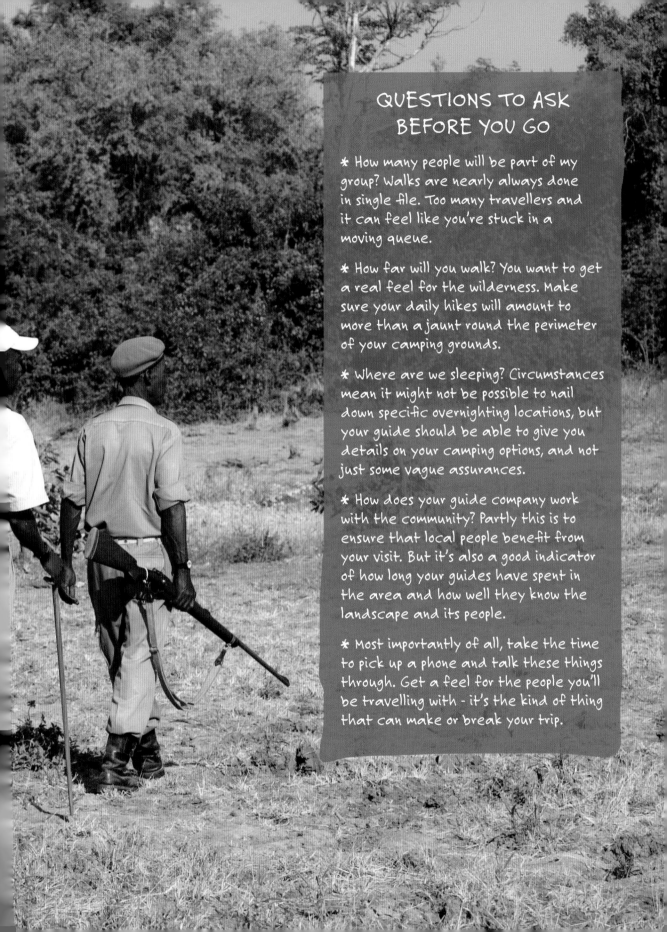

QUESTIONS TO ASK BEFORE YOU GO

* How many people will be part of my group? Walks are nearly always done in single file. Too many travellers and it can feel like you're stuck in a moving queue.

* How far will you walk? You want to get a real feel for the wilderness. Make sure your daily hikes will amount to more than a jaunt round the perimeter of your camping grounds.

* Where are we sleeping? Circumstances mean it might not be possible to nail down specific overnighting locations, but your guide should be able to give you details on your camping options, and not just some vague assurances.

* How does your guide company work with the community? Partly this is to ensure that local people benefit from your visit. But it's also a good indicator of how long your guides have spent in the area and how well they know the landscape and its people.

* Most importantly of all, take the time to pick up a phone and talk these things through. Get a feel for the people you'll be travelling with - it's the kind of thing that can make or break your trip.

MORE ENCOUNTERS WITH NATURE

KALIMANTAN, INDONESIA

The island of Borneo is the last great stronghold for orangutans. While most people go to the Malaysian provinces of Sabah and Sarawak on the north of the island, the smart choice is to head for the Indonesian province of Kalimantan to the south. Tanjung Puting National Park is far less easy to get to and hosts only a fraction of the visitors. Your reward for making the uncomfortable journey by boat to this remote spot is the chance to walk with one of the largest remaining populations of orangutans. An estimated 5,000 live in the area and with any luck you'll see them in their natural habitat on a guided jungle walk or by traversing one of the narrow rivers which snake through the park. If you're very fortunate, you might be able to book a tour with Dr Birute Mary Galdikas, whose pioneering research in the region has done a lot to increase our knowledge of 'The Old Man of the Forest'.

DEMOCRATIC REPUBLIC OF THE CONGO

An encounter with mountain gorillas will set your pulse racing and live long in your memory.

MANITOBA, CANADA

The frozen tundra of Canada's far north is the domain of the polar bear. A walking safari across the ice allows you a chance to share the wild with these magnificent predators. The best time to visit is the autumn when the bears lurk around the shores of Hudson Bay, waiting for the waters to freeze so they can hunt seals. Most of the time your encounters will be at long-range but every so often a nosey bear will come over for a closer look.

The experience of watching a 1,000 pound predator mosey towards you is both exhilarating and terrifying. Your guides let the bears come close – but not too close. They employ a range of techniques if your walk is in danger of becoming a bit bitey, including talking quietly but firmly to the bear; blowing an air horn and firing harmless cap guns in the air. One of these measures nearly always does the trick. If not, a warning shot from your guide's shotgun will see your new furry friend lose interest very quickly. Sometimes the best view of a polar bear is watching it turn tail and jog away.

ASSAM, INDIA

Kaziranga National Park isn't the biggest reserve in India, and it doesn't have the same profile as some of the country's other nature spots, but it's the kind of place where you might just get lucky on a walking safari. The abundance of wildlife is mind-boggling: for starters, this is home to two-thirds of the world's Indian One-Horned rhinoceros and more than half the world's wild water buffalo. There's a healthy number of Bengal tigers and around 2,000 Asian elephants. Your chances of seeing some of them are pretty good and you never know, if you get the right guides and tread carefully, you might see the lot. Native grasses as tall as humans are one of Kaziranga's hallmarks, which means an experienced guide is critical if you want to make the most of your visit (and avoid becoming a tiger's lunch).

MAGNIFICENT SEVEN

Adventures on the roof of the world

At the summit you allow yourself a few moments of pure satisfaction; a quick look at the markers left there by the climbers who have preceded you, a couple of photos and a brief celebration with your climbing partners.

You have literally reached the pinnacle. It's taken years of training, planning, sacrifice, study, saving and travelling (did we mention training?) to get to this point.

This is a test which makes unique demands of anyone who chooses to take

it. You've conquered some of the toughest climbs on Earth; you've gasped for oxygen in the thin air at the roof of the world; you've been to places where barely a handful of humans have been before.

Your journey has taken you across frozen Antarctic wastes and through dense, uninhabited jungle. You've flirted with war zones and tramped across deserts.

It's the challenge of a lifetime. And it all starts with acknowledging one simple truth... sometimes size isn't everything.

THE SECOND SEVEN SUMMITS

Climbing the Seven Summits – the highest point on each continent – is an increasingly well-known extreme adventure challenge. But there's a greater buzz to be had by looking at what's next on the list. The second highest peaks are just as much of a test as their big brothers and, in some cases, much, much harder. Only the most accomplished mountain men and women will be able to get seven ticks on this list.

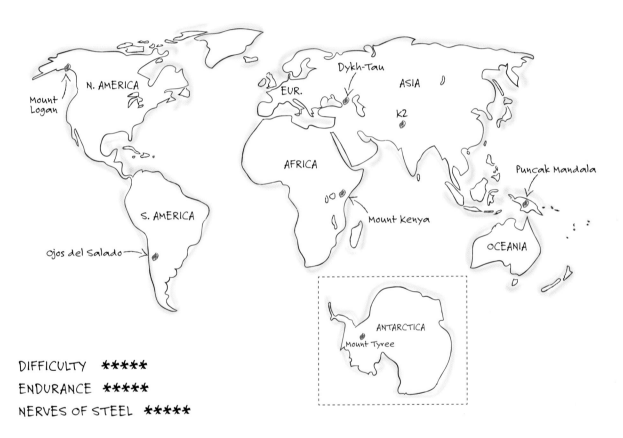

DIFFICULTY *****
ENDURANCE *****
NERVES OF STEEL *****

DURATION: WHO KNOWS?
PERSONNEL: A CLIMB TEAM OF AT LEAST FOUR, SUPPORTED BY GROUND CREW
SKILLSET: WORLD-CLASS ALPINE CLIMBING TECHNIQUE,
             EXPERIENCE OF HIGH-ALTITUDE ACTIVITY,
             A PERSONABLE MANNER TO SOLICIT DONATIONS AND SPONSORSHIP
RISKS: ALTITUDE SICKNESS, HYPOTHERMIA, FROSTBITE,
             AVALANCHES, ROCK FALLS, EXHAUSTION

In the big book of legendary mountain figures, few names burn brighter than Reinhold Messner's. An Italian from the German-speaking province of South Tyrol, his achievements are truly staggering. Messner climbed Mount Everest without supplementary oxygen when few believed this was humanly possible. Planet Earth has 14 peaks higher than 8,000 metres ('8000ers'); Messner was the first human to climb them all. He has pioneered routes on monstrous rock faces that no climber has been able to replicate. And, just for good measure, in 1990 Messner and his walking partner Arved Fuchs became the first people to cross Antarctica without the support of snowmobiles or dog sleds.

THE SEVEN SUMMITS

Asia – Everest (29,035 feet)
South America – Aconcagua (22,834 feet)
North America – Denali (20,310 feet)
Africa – Kilimanjaro (19,340 feet)
Europe – Elbrus (18,513 feet)
Antarctica – Vinson (16,067 feet)
Oceania – Puncak Jaya (16,023 feet)

One of Messner's lasting legacies has been to raise the profile of one of mountaineering's toughest challenges – the Seven Summits. The concept of climbing the highest peak on each of Earth's continents was first put forward by an American called Dick Bass.

Messner was intrigued by Bass's idea but, perhaps unsurprisingly, thought it wasn't tough enough. At just 7,310 ft and with no discernible climbing or scrambling challenges to speak of, Mount Kosciuszko in Australia was something of a let-down. Messner fixed this by swapping it out for Puncak Jaya in New Guinea, which is part of the same continental plate as Australia and an infinitely tougher test. Messner didn't just talk the talk. He walked the walk, and climbed the climb, by becoming the second person to complete the new, tougher Seven Summits list (a Canadian called Pat Morrow was the first, in case you're wondering).

THE SECOND SEVEN

Since then the Seven Summits concept has taken root and become an increasingly popular adventure for experienced mountaineers. Perhaps a bit *too* popular for some tastes. Several tour organizers will sell you a Seven Summits training package and assist with sorting your trips to each of the mountains. While not exactly on a par with an all-inclusive package holiday on a beach somewhere, the Seven Summits is now a well-established part of the extreme adventure circuit.

Then there's the mountains themselves. Of the seven, a skilled alpinist is only going to be challenged by a couple of peaks on the list. Everest's sheer height makes huge physical demands on the body but the route to the summit on the Nepalese side is well-worn. Puncak Jaya is a tough proposition, but Kilimanjaro, Vinson, Elbrus, Aconcagua and Denali are strenuous hikes rather than complicated climbs.

The accessibility of these high peaks means that, by 2016, more than 400 people had completed the Seven Summits, following either Bass or Messner's lists. Some critics now say the Seven Summits is more a measure of financial clout than courage and skill.

What if you're the kind of person who wants something a bit more niche? Fortunately, the solution is staring you right in the face.

Mount Kenya

In 2013 an Austrian called Christian Stangl completed the Second Seven Summits. The idea of climbing the second highest point on each continent had been discussed in mountaineering circles for some time. Stangl went out and did it.

The logic is as fairly simple. None of the 'second' peaks are easier to scale and most are more difficult – hellishly more difficult in at least one case. Take Africa. Kilimanjaro is a long but straightforward slog to the top. Mount Kenya is a far sharper peak which requires proper rock climbing. It's the same story in Europe, where Dykh-Tau in the Russian Caucasus range is a far greater technical examination than nearby Mount Elbrus.

THE 2ND SEVEN SUMMITS

Asia – K2 (28,251 feet)
South America – Ojos del Salado (22,608 feet)
North America – Logan (19,551 feet)
Africa – Kenya (17,057 feet)
Europe – Dykh-Tau (17,077 feet)
Antarctica – Tyree (15,919 feet)
Oceania – Puncak Mandala (15,580 feet)

K2

Denali and Mount Logan in North America present very similar challenges – both demand serious consideration if you attempt them in winter – but the route to Mount Logan is much harder to access and therefore more difficult.

There's not much to choose between the relative tests offered by Aconcagua and Ojos del Salado in South America but, once you've knocked those four off your list, the fun really starts.

Puncak Jaya, jutting out of the New Guinea jungle, is a tough climb but slightly shorter Puncak Mandala is even harder, not least because you have to hack through some very nasty, oppressive tropical forest for several days before you can even think about your ascent.

Then there's Mount Tyree, Antarctica's second top spot. Getting there is rough. Climbing it is even rougher, requiring polished technique in one of Earth's most inhospitable environments. By 2017 only six climbing parties, and fifteen people, had made it to the summit. Fifteen. Barely enough to scrape together a rugby team.

THE SAVAGE MOUNTAIN

Then there's the big one. The Savage Mountain – K2. At 28,251 ft, it's shorter than Everest (29,029 ft), but nobody doubts which peak presents the deadlier challenge. For a start, it's tucked away in the nether regions of the Karakoram Range, one of the most inaccessible and hostile places on Earth. Then there's the unrelenting nature of the ascent. Climbers on K2 experience the same altitude and weather problems of Everest but have to negotiate a far more demanding route to the summit.

The human cost is ferocious. Only around 300 people have successfully summited. Seventy-seven people have died in the attempt, which

means that for every five people who head out for the top, only four come back.

No part of the K2 challenge is straightforward but things get real at 17,400 ft above sea level, the starting point of the notorious Abruzzi Spur on the mountain's southeast ridge. It says much for the alternatives that this prominent lump of ice, rock and snow is seen as the best option of making it to the summit, because it will test every sinew of the climbers who take it on.

Initially, there's House's Chimney, a narrow chute ascending 100 ft which was first climbed in 1938 by Bill House from the US. The addition of fixed ropes has reduced the risk but it still demands respect.

THE BLACK PYRAMID

After setting up camp at the top of the Chimney, the Ridge's next demand is the ominously named Black Pyramid. An expert could spend days explaining the technicalities of the rock and ice climbs, the punishing overhangs and the stress it places on your body but it all boils down to one thing – uncertainty. The Black Pyramid section is 1,200 ft long and much of its cliffs are covered in slabs of snow. At any point a big chunk of white stuff could slip away and leave you with a world of problems. You can be confident that the snow on the route you have chosen won't give way – but you can never be absolutely certain. Over the course of the Black Pyramid, this uncertainty takes its toll on the minds of even the most resolute of characters.

The mental torture continues the next day. After another night in camp, climbers head into a narrow valley which funnels wind directly into your face and makes the slopes on either side prone to avalanches. An avalanche at 24,000 ft is more than likely to put a sharp end to any summit attempt.

HOW DID K2 GET ITS NAME?

Nothing sums up the stark, blunt challenge of an assault on K2 better than the mountain's name itself. A British surveyor who arrived to take measurements of the Karakoram in 1856 saw two massive peaks about 130 miles to his south and noted them as K1 and K2. K1 turned out be known locally as Masherbrum. K2 didn't have a name. It was so remote there was no one around to give it a title. Mount Godwen-Austen was suggested, after a British explorer, but it was rejected by the Royal Geographical Society. So the no nonsense moniker of K2 – literally Karakoram 2 – has stuck. Suits it perfectly.

Baltoro Glacier,
Karakoram Range.
Caravan of porters,
trekkers & climbers

Next up is The Shoulder. It starts at 25,225 ft and, unlike House's Chimney and the Black Pyramid, has to be climbed without fixed ropes. A thick layer of ice and snow means there is no exact route through the terrain, only a general direction which should be followed. This means trial and error, and trusting your brain to operate with precision despite being starved of oxygen at high altitude. Your reward for overcoming The Shoulder is a cold, breathless night at a final camp before a crack at the summit.

You set off well before dawn. This final ascent is the hardest challenge of the entire Second Summits adventure. The lack of oxygen slows your body and addles your mind; there's no hiding place from the ferocity of the wind or the extreme cold. At 26,900 ft, you reach The Bottleneck, where falling chunks of an overhanging ice cliff can rain down on you at any moment. Get through The Bottleneck and you'll make it on to the final summit ridge, which is no place to hang about, either. Here the gale-force winds can sweep you clean off the mountain while the icy surface makes for treacherous progress.

At the summit itself you look down on the mighty Karakoram range. But there's barely time to take stock of what you've achieved and absolutely no room for complacency. The downward journey is scarcely less threatening

than the upward route and will require every last ounce of your remaining physical and mental resources.

So there it is. The Second Seven Summits. The challenge of a lifetime. And let's be honest, it's a challenge which is going to be beyond the skills, budget and physical capacity of almost everyone.

But the spirit behind the Second Summits challenge – to seek out an adventure based on the merit of the challenge, rather than the hype that surrounds it – is something that will stand you in good stead for other adventures.

THE SEVEN VOLCANIC SUMMITS

Asia – Damavand (18,406 feet)
South America – Ojas del Salado (22,608 feet)
North America – Pico de Orizaba (18,491 feet)
Africa – Kilimanjaro (19,340 feet)
Europe – Elbrus (18,513 feet)
Antarctica – Sidley (14,058 feet)
Oceania – Giluwe (14,331 feet)

THE LOST HIGHWAY

Climbing K2 is one hell of a challenge. Getting there isn't any picnic either. It's in the heart of the Karakoram, one of the wildest, least accessible places in the world. Early attempts to climb the mountain were hindered by the need to ship in astonishing amounts of provisions from distant towns to support the climbing party and their porters.

Things have got a bit easier since then, but not much. If you do find yourself lucky enough to have a crack at K2, your introduction to the Karakoram Range should include a journey along one of the world's great roads. The N-35, more widely known as the Karakoram Highway or KKH for short, threads its way through the mountains for more than 800 miles

Passu Cathedral,
Northern Pakistan

between the Punjab in Pakistan and Xinjiang in China.

Along the way, the KKH brushes past no fewer than five '8,000ers' and countless other majestic peaks and through the stunning Hunza Valley, a quiet oasis of green wedged between pinnacles of snow and rock. Security concerns in Pakistan mean the KKH really is a road less travelled, sadly, but if you do decide to take the high road, it's a journey that will live on in your mind forever.

RING OF FIRE CIRCUIT

In addition to the Seven Summits, and the Second Seven Summits, another established list in mountaineering circles is the Seven Volcanic Summits. It is, surprise, surprise, a challenge to scale the highest volcanic peaks on each continent. But while the concept sounds intriguing, the list itself is not. It includes Kilimanjaro and Elbrus, two of the least interesting Seven Summits; Mount Sidley in Antarctica, which is so remote it might as well be on the Moon, and most of the volcanoes aren't very, well, volcanoey. There hasn't been an eruption on Elbrus, for instance, in nearly 2,000 years. So why not create a challenge which keeps the cool volcano bit but ditches the dullness?

The Pacific Ocean is surrounded by an area of wild tectonic activity known as the Ring of Fire. On a map it looks like a massive crescent, arcing from New Zealand, through East Asia and Northwest America, to the foot of the Andes in South America. More than 80 percent of the world's large earthquakes occur in this zone. It's also where you find many of the world's active volcanoes. And lots of them are well worth a climb. So, without further ado and heading in a clockwise direction, here is the Pacific Rim Seven:

MOUNT GILUWE, PAPUA NEW GUINEA (14,331 FEET)

The tallest volcanic peak in the Oceania region, Mount Giluwe is located in the Southern Highlands of Papua New Guinea. Its jagged twin peaks jut out from the surrounding forest in spectacular fashion and the route to the top encompasses dramatic shifts in flora and fauna as the altitude changes.

MOUNT MAYON, PHILIPPINES (8,081 FEET)

If someone says the word 'volcano' to you, the image that pops into your head is probably a perfect conical peak, rising from level ground, with a plume of smoke puffing out the top. Well, you've just pictured Mayon Volcano. It's a thing of beauty, just begging to be climbed. This peak on the Philippine island of Luzon is very active so you'll need to keep a close eye on seismic reports unless you fancy a bath in liquid hot lava.

MOUNT FUJI, JAPAN (12,389 FEET)

Mount Fuji, just 60 miles southwest of central Tokyo, isn't just a volcano – it's an icon. For centuries it's been an emblem of Japan and its culture. Try to visit in the shoulder season of May or September when the bitter cold is worth dealing with to avoid the summer crowds. Do what the locals do and aim to summit just before sunrise for a stunning start to the day.

KLYUCHEVSKAYA SOPKA, RUSSIA (15,584 FEET)

The Kamchatka Peninsula in Siberia is, literally, a hotbed of seismic activity. Geysers spout from the ground, the earth wobbles with regular quakes and the

Mount Fuji

area is designated a World Heritage Site by UNESCO for being one of the "most outstanding volcanic regions in the world". Klyuchevskaya Sopka is the tallest active volcano in the Northern Hemisphere and is a demanding but rewarding climb in one of the world's great wildernesses.

PICO DE ORIZABA, MEXICO (18,491 FEET)

The highest volcanic peak in North and Central America, Pico de Orizaba, strikes a spectacular profile when seen from the flat plains which surround it. Despite its tropical location, the summit is constantly covered in a cap of ice and some routes can require a reasonable degree of technical ice climbing ability.

CHIMBORAZO, ECUADOR (20,548 FEET)

This dormant volcano in the Ecuadorian Andes isn't the tallest mountain in the world – not even close – but by summiting here you will have earned the distinction of being as far from the centre of the earth as a human can get on land. It's only one degree south of the equator and due to Earth's curvature, it's actually 7,000 feet further from the core than Mount Everest. So there.

OJOS DEL SALADO, CHILE/ARGENTINA (22,615 FEET)

The last Pacific Rim peak is the world's tallest volcano. Ojos del Salado, on the border between Chile and Argentina, also features in the Second Seven Summits list. Although there has been no recorded eruption for more than 1,000 years, Ojos del Salado surprised everyone by puffing out some plumes of ash in the early 1990s.

"Going on an adventure is a way of slowing down time. So many people reach retirement and wonder where their last forty years went. You don't have to chuck your job, just find adventure as often as you can."

SOURCE TO SEA
Exploration

This must be the place. It's not much to look at, a shallow hole in the ground with a small trickle of water seeping out, but it represents something so much bigger. After weeks of searching, scouring acres of remote countryside, you've finally found the source. This tiny pulse will turn into a trace, then a stream and will keep gathering and growing until it's a mighty river. A flicker of doubt crosses your mind for the briefest moment. Perhaps there's a further point in some other direction?

A scan of the landscape confirms that this high ground is the only realistic spot in which your river could start. What's more, the indigenous people who visit this area – and know it better than anyone – are convinced. So the doubt is booted from your mind and replaced with a different feeling: anticipation. You're about to start the next phase of your expedition and it's going to take you through some of the most magical territory you'll ever see. All you have to do is keep heading downstream.

PADDLE THE ESSEQUIBO RIVER, GUYANA

Hike to the source of the Essequibo River in Guyana, South America, and follow its course 630 miles north to the point where it empties into the Atlantic Ocean. On the way you'll paddle through an untouched wilderness of indescribable beauty.

DIFFICULTY ★★★★★

ENDURANCE ★★★★★

NERVES OF STEEL ★★★★★

DURATION:	BEST ADVICE? COUNT UP THE WEEKS YOU THINK YOU'LL NEED – THEN DOUBLE IT
PERSONNEL:	TWO OR THREE, PLUS LOCAL GUIDES AND SUPPORT
SKILLSET:	PADDLING TECHNIQUE, NAVIGATION, BUSHCRAFT
RISKS:	DROWNING, ANIMAL ATTACK, TROPICAL ILLNESS

Atlantic Ocean

Anna Regina

Finish

Georgetown

New Amsterdam

Cuyuni

VENEZUELA

Mazaruni

Essequibo

Linden

Pakaraima Mtns

GUYANA

Essequibo

SURINAME

BRAZIL

Kunuku Mts

Village on the Essequibo

Essequibo

N

0   80 miles

Kamoa Mts

Sipu

Acarai Mts

BRAZIL

Start

You never forget your first encounter with a jaguar. Only a few thousand of these magnificent jungle predators remain, camouflaged in the depths of some of Earth's wildest places. Their habitat has been squeezed as the modern world encroaches. It's sadly no surprise that a jaguar's natural reaction to an approaching human is to turn tail and make for the safety of the forest. Encounters on foot are incredibly rare as a result. But when you're travelling on water, the rules change, and a whole new set of opportunities open up to you.

Trekking through the jungle to reach the source

furthest source of the Essequibo is several weeks' worth of proper jungle exploring. That means checking trees for spiders, scorpions and other wildlife as you hack your way through; tapping logs before stepping over them to avoid any unwanted encounters; and taking measures to make sure you never find yourself alone with a jaguar. Yes, we know you want to see one but it's safer to have your machete to hand if your wish comes true. And never wander off alone in an area where there are signs of big cat activity.

It's a great feeling when you find the river's origin, but it doesn't change the fact that there's still a lot of work to do before you take to the water. The early stages of the tributary you're following are a long, exhausting natural obstacle course. Fallen branches and upturned trunks block your path – there's no way you can navigate a kayak through this section of the river. It's slow and physically demanding work but every day the water course widens a little as you make progress until, finally, you can take to your craft.

You'll almost certainly be using an inflatable kayak as it has several massive advantages for a trip like this. It's light, which means it sits on top of the water beautifully and is easy to direct. It tends to bounce off boulders on impact, so it will negotiate rapids without making a huge fuss of every bump. Finally, it folds up neatly, which means the inflatable boat can come with you on the plane and is easily portaged past waterfalls or unnegotiable rapids. They're good and roomy, too.

The only real downside is also caused by its lack of weight; the inflatable craft is susceptible to being blown about by the strong gusts of wind. That's not really a problem during the early stages of your journey. Thick forests flank the river banks and shelter you from severe weather.

In your kayak you can glide along with minimal fuss and very little noise; you can merge with the surroundings in a way that just isn't possible on foot. That means there's a chance, maybe, that one day as you progress through a world of vivid greens, you might look to the riverbank and see the distinctive black-on-tan markings of the largest cat in the Americas. You'll get little more than a moment together but it's enough to sear an indelible mark in your memory.

SETTING OUT FROM THE SOURCE

Before your river adventure begins, there is the not-so-small matter of getting to the starting point – an adventure in itself. Cutting a trail through Guyana's rainforest to get to the

Essequibo River

AN ANIMAL KINGDOM

After the exertion of your hike through the forest, the first few days on the water are bliss. You're in a realm of great beauty, surrounded by nature, and you've got the place pretty much to yourself. It can feel like you've stepped back to an earlier age altogether – at times you almost expect a dinosaur to burst through the thick foliage. Instead, there's a regular accompaniment of contemporary creatures such as capuchin and howler monkeys, fruit bats and black caimans – a member of the crocodile family that can grow to 20 ft in length.

Again, thanks to the assistance of the current, it's possible to take in more of the events around you than it would be if you were travelling on foot. Sure, there's hard work to be done, but there's also scope to sit back and soak up your environs at times, even while you're on the move.

One area where you're certainly not going to relax is when you're having to negotiate rough rapids. You'll have to know how to read water if you want to get from A to B through the toughest stretches. The key is to see beyond the rapids and be mindful of what's waiting for you beyond the lively water; if the water continues to flow ahead in a straightforward manner, it's usually safe to proceed. If the rapids are followed by an ominous, swirling pool of deep water, that should spark a danger alert in your mind. There's a very real chance you could get sucked into the depths. Over time your senses will become heightened to risk and adept at identifying what's possible – and what's not – but the golden rule never changes. If you're not sure of the water ahead, don't put yourself into it.

NEW PLACES TO DISCOVER?

Sometimes it might feel as if there aren't many unknown parts of this world left to explore. Satellites capture images of every nook and cranny; human expansion has stretched into untouched wilderness; and increased access to transportation has made it easier than ever before to head into previously inaccessible territories.

But there are still big-scale expeditions to be enjoyed – if you know where to look. In 2018, a group of British adventurers proved this point. They found the furthest source of Guyana's longest river, the Essequibo, and followed the water course all the way to the sea, a journey of more than 600 miles.

The three-woman team – Laura Bingham, Pip Stewart and Ness Knight (pictured, left to right, above) – took 10 weeks to complete their mission. Working with the indigenous Wai Wai people, it took three weeks of scouring the Acarai Mountains, near Guyana's border with Brazil, to reach the river's origin. Then they had to use chainsaws, axes and machetes to cut their way through no fewer than 162 obstacles before the river became navigable by kayak. Only then could the expedition take to the water and start the long paddle to the shores of the Atlantic Ocean.

Along the way, the group experienced encounters with black caiman, piranha, and a jaguar, which wandered into their camp one night.

Laura Bingham's advice for anyone planning to follow in their footsteps? Don't become discouraged by the extensive preparation. "The hardest thing about an expedition like this was getting to the starting line," she says. "There's a lot of red tape to deal with and permissions to get. A lot of the area we travelled through was protected and we had to get approval from all the villages that we'd contact down river. It took time."

And the best thing? "It's such an enormous privilege to travel through such an untouched paradise. It's like Eden."

Close to its confluence with the Atlantic Ocean, the Essequibo river is a few miles wide

HUMAN IMPACT

You've been living in nature for several days, perhaps even weeks, paddling during the day, camping near the river at night. So it's all the more jarring when you come across signs of human activity. The government of Guyana has taken steps to limit the impact of logging and mineral extraction from the country's rainforests but you'll still come across activity that feels completely at odds with the natural realm you've cruised through. By this point you are starting to fixate on your final destination, the delta region and the point at which the Essequibo enters the Atlantic Ocean.

You've travelled more than 600 miles and pulled back the curtain on a world of incredible natural diversity. When it stops it's going to take some time to process the whole experience. Once you have, it's likely you'll be left with a thirst for more. Now, where's that map...?

OTHER RIVERS TO EXPLORE

IRRAWADDY RIVER, MYANMAR (BURMA)

This mighty river comes to life at the confluence of the Mali and Nmai rivers, near the border with China, and surges south for more than 1,300 miles. A source-to-sea adventure here will transport you through the heart of Myanmar, past gorges, forests and plains, before bringing you to the tropical shores of the Andaman Sea. The river's upper reaches are characterized by three dramatic 'defiles', narrow passages where the water is squeezed between steep-sided riverbanks, while the lower sections incorporate a large delta system where you might catch a glimpse of an Irrawaddy Dolphin or two.

MURRAY RIVER, AUSTRALIA

The Murray is Australia's longest river, measuring 1,558 miles from its source in the Australian Alps to its mouth in the Indian Ocean. You won't find much in the way of waterfalls or rapids on this journey. Instead of white water you'll experience pure tranquillity. Unlike many long rivers, the Murray's banks are not particularly steep-sided, which means for long stretches you'll have great views of Australia's vast open spaces as you glide along. Watch out for 'snags' – dead gum trees which float on, or sometimes just under, the surface of the water.

Murray river

HOME ALONE

Live off-grid

It's a tempting thought that has passed through the mind of many an adventurous traveller. You've been hiking along through a pleasingly empty bit of countryside when you reach a vantage point and, quite suddenly, have a moment of clarity. A glorious view, completely devoid of any sign of human activity, unfolds itself in front of you. A lively river burbles away, flanked by a decent smattering of mature woodland. There

are abundant signs of animal life and a rolling landscape to offer some protection from the worst excesses of the weather. The four basic requirements for survival are food, water, shelter and fire, and you have access to all of them right here.

And so that enticing, tantalising notion worms its way into your head: "could I make a go of living here?" There really is only one way to find out.

NORTH WOODS, MAINE, USA

Let's get one thing clear. There's a big difference between surviving and living. Surviving is about doing enough to make it from one day to the next by whatever means necessary. Living, which is what you'll be trying to do on this adventure in the natural beauty of Maine, is something altogether different. It's about making a life for yourself that can be sustained through the changing seasons for months, years... maybe even decades.

DIFFICULTY **★★★★**★

ENDURANCE **★★★**★★

NERVES OF STEEL **★★★**★★

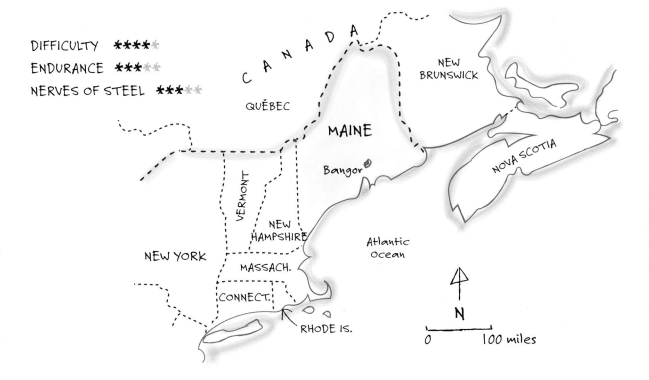

DURATION: AT LEAST 4 SEASONS

PERSONNEL: YOU (AND FRIENDS OR FAMILY IF YOU WANT/CAN CONVINCE THEM TO JOIN YOU)

SKILLSET: ANIMAL-TENDING, WOOD WORKING, CONSTRUCTION, HUNTING, GARDENING

RISKS: STARVATION, ISOLATION-INDUCED STRESS

Making a home for yourself in the wilds is about investing in yourself. It's about seeing if you've got the ability, the resolve and the resourcefulness to provide everything you need to carve out a living. It's highly unlikely you'll have all the skills required when you start out. You'll need to learn as you go, develop your craftsmanship, expand your knowledge and strengthen your mind. Whether you choose to go off-grid for a specific amount of time or to make it an open-ended venture, you'll be giving yourself a set of skills that will serve you well in any walk

of life; an innate confidence that, whatever the circumstances you find yourself in, you'll be able to absorb, adapt and move on.

The first decision you need to make is where to set up your homestead. There are certain considerations that should bear heavily on your decision. Decent natural resources, availability of land and a fairly relaxed regulatory regime should be among your priorities. Reliable rainfall and a ripe growing season should also be factors.

The American state of Maine is an inviting option. It covers more than 35,000 square miles and more than 90 percent of the state's population live in a narrow band within 15 miles of the coast. That means there's a massive, empty interior in which to make your home.

When it comes to off-grid living, this is a state with many advantages. Land is relatively inexpensive. Building regulations allow for non-standard construction in rural areas, which means you shouldn't have any problems in getting permission for a self-built log cabin. Rainfall is plentiful, which means you are rarely likely to run dry, and generally rich soil and long summers make for decent crop-growing conditions.

And to top it all there's Maine's trump card: wood. It's the most heavily forested state in America, so your land is likely to be well-stocked with timber for building, burning and crafting.

What are the drawbacks? The chief downside of choosing a state in the farthest

northeastern reaches of the United States is the winter weather. It can get brutally cold and heavy snowfall is almost guaranteed. If you plan to grow crops or maintain livestock, you'll need to devise a workable plan to manage your resources through the coldest months.

LIFE'S ESSENTIALS

Once you've homed in on a location for your off-grid stronghold, you need to make your mind up about a few general principles. Are you going to strip things right back to basics and live without any of the trappings of the modern world whatsoever? Or are you going to incorporate up-to-date gadgetry to make your life slightly easier?

Take power, for instance. Advances in technology mean that usable renewable energy sources are more accessible than ever before. Low-impact solar panel systems, for instance, are easy to install and manage, and provide a reliable source of power except in the very darkest depths of winter. Then again, solar can be expensive, and humans have managed to live quite happily for thousands of years without access to such things – many still do. Is a power source really necessary?

To a certain extent, it comes down to personal choice and what you hope to get out of your independent living experience. The longer you plan on staying, the more sense it makes to think about how sustainable your way of life will be.

BASIC TIPS FOR BUILDING YOUR LOG CABIN

* If you can, use dry, dead wood. This will be much less work than taking a living tree, which is heavier because of the water weight. Inspect the logs to ensure they don't have insects or rot inside.

* Take your time and plan the design. Don't make it up as you go along. If you think you might extend in the future, plan ahead.

* Orientate your cabin so that the prevailing wind isn't headed straight for your front door. Keep the number of windows down to a minimum and put them on the leeward side. Don't put too many sun-facing windows in, or you'll bake in the summer.

* Don't be tempted to cut down lots of trees around the cabin, as they will act as a windbreak and provide a lot of shade. Deciduous trees to the south of the cabin won't have leaves in the winter so you'll get the sun. In summer, the leaves will protect you from too much of it.

* Try to create rooms that have more than one purpose.

* Locate your cabin close to water, but not too close!

Once you've found a spot in the Maine backcountry and worked out in your head what the rules of this challenge will be, it's time to turn your attention to the four essentials of survival: shelter, fire, water and food.

You'll want to build your own shelter, otherwise – honestly – what's the point? The mighty northern white cedar is what you're looking for here. It's hard enough to make a solid building but soft enough to be able to fit into shape. With a bit of practice, it's entirely possible to create a decent-sized cabin without using a single nail. Don't obsess about the size of your dwelling. Bigger isn't necessarily better and the amount of space you require, without all the usual equipment of modern life or the prospects of guests to entertain, is pretty limited. Focus instead on making sure it's wind and watertight and is easy to heat.

To heat your new home, you'll need the means of making a fire and a safe place to start a blaze. You're in one of the woodiest spots on the continental United States, so the first bit's not a problem. The second part can be much more difficult. Do yourself a favour and bring a small wood-burning stove. You may need permission from a local authority, depending on the by-laws of the area where you settle, but this is one short-cut that is definitely worth taking.

With your lodgings sorted, you'll now want to focus on water. Maine has it in abundance and, sometimes, when the rain is sweeping in off the Atlantic Ocean, you might wish there was a little bit less! Nothing is more important to the success of your venture than having access to a reliable source of clean water. The best option is to obtain a piece of land with a river or stream running through it but, failing that, a hand-operated pump to draw water from a well or aquifer should do the trick. Check the local regulations, though. You'll almost certainly have rights to use water from your land for personal consumption, but using it to water crops or sustain animals may be a different matter.

Talking of animals... the fourth essential for survival is food. And here, we come back to the difference between surviving and living. It is possible to hunt and forage for sustenance for a sustained period of time but don't underestimate how soul-sapping it can be to eat the same staples day after day. Consider whether you can incorporate keeping a few animals and growing some vegetables into your plan. Having some chickens and a goat for eggs and milk massively increases your dining options and ensures you have a ready supply of protein, while the local climate is pretty good for growing crops such as carrots and kale.

THRIVING

Once you've taken steps to ensure you have the means to survive, it's time to focus on an element of independent living that's sometimes overlooked, the 'living' part. There's so much more to life than the bare essentials. It would be naïve to think you don't need more if you're planning to spend an extended period of time by yourself. You might be going off-grid but you'll still have a brain in your head that needs some kind of stimulation. This isn't supposed to be an ordeal, it's supposed to be a route to a better way of being. Think about how you're going to make the most of your downtime. Books, crafting, exercise, meditation – you're giving yourself a chance to broaden your mind and deepen your spirit. If you are successful, it might seem like you're the last man, or woman, on Earth... and it will feel just fine.

OR LIVE IN A CAVE

YUKON, CANADA

If finding a plot of land and building your own shelter doesn't necessarily float your boat, why not try a slightly different form of off-grid living? People have been making caves their homes for thousands of years. There are some places, such as in Turkey, Spain and Iran, where they still do.

The rugged Yukon territory of northwestern Canada is a paradise for would-be troglodytes. The forests are a good source of food; there's moose and deer to be hunted, and mushrooms to be foraged. The Yukon River can be fished, when it isn't frozen over.

There are two essentials you'll need to take care of right away if you're going to have a crack at cave living. First, you need to put a door on the place to keep out bracing winds and curious animals. Second, you need to sort out a way to heat the place. Yukon winters are deadly; if you don't have a heat source and fuel to fire it, you're not going to make it.

A properly-insulated cave will be cool in summer and cosy in winter – and stone walls require very little maintenance.

Check for any troublesome squatters before selecting a cave

A FINAL WORD

This is the end of the book but, hopefully, the start of many new adventures. The challenges set out in these pages are examples of places to go and thrills to experience but, remember, they are examples. Your own travel ambitions might be very different but the most important thing about adventure is also the most simple: get up and go.

Don't wait for everything to be perfect. Don't wait until you have every answer to every doubt. You'll learn to cope when things aren't perfect; you'll discover that there isn't an answer to every doubt (and that a lot of the doubts were only ever a trick of the mind to start with). The one thing you can't do is find out these things without leaving your comfort zone and taking a step into the unknown.

What are you waiting for?

Ed Stafford

"The person who risks nothing, does nothing, has nothing, is nothing, and becomes nothing. He may avoid suffering and sorrow, but he simply cannot learn, feel, change, grow or love.

Chained by his certitude, he is a slave; he has forfeited his freedom.

Only the person who risks is truly free."

Leo F. Buscaglia

INDEX OF ENTRIES BY COUNTRY

Page numbers refer to the opening page of the category. Page numbers in bold refer to the main entry.

ACKNOWLEDGEMENTS

While every effort has been made to trace the owner of copyright material reproduced herein and secure permission, the publishers would like to apologize for any omission and will be pleased to incorporate missing acknowledgements in any future edition of this book.

Ed Stafford would like to thank the following individuals and organisations for their help in creating this book:

Assistance with specific entries:

Steven Reynolds: A HEAD FOR HEIGHTS
Richard Boddington:
    SURF AND TURF & HELL OR WHITE WATER
Lewis Pugh (lewispugh.com): FROZEN WATER
Dibin Devassy (artofbicycletrips.com): LIFE CYCLE
Ben Jamin (kombilife.com): THE OPEN ROAD
Fiona McIntosh: INTO THE ABYSS
Colin Arisman (wildconfluence.com):
    WALK THE WORLD
Bob Gair: A KITE IN THE WIND
Angus MacGregor: MAKE TRACKS
Sifter-writes-bikes.blogspot.com: MAKE TRACKS
Laura Bingham (laurabingham.org):
    SOURCE TO SEA

Special thanks to Ed Tilston and the team at Jaguar Land Rover, Coventry, for their input.

Thanks also to Peter Hennessey, Malcolm Parry, Moira Rowbotham, Jillian Paterson, Tim Frings and David Wardale for their assistance.

Origination and Design

I would like to thank Mark Steward and Alan Greenwood for their editorial services.

Project management, editorial, design and typesetting: Pixo Creative Services (www.pixocreative.com)

Additional editorial services:
    Richard Happer; Karen Midgely

HarperCollins Publishers

Text editing and proof reading:
    Hannah MacAskill

I would also like to thank Jethro Lennox and the team in Glasgow.

p103, Rapid classification (rivervalley.co.nz)

PHOTO CREDITS

SS: Shutterstock.com
CC 2.0: Creative Commons Attribution Licence 2.0 Generic

© as follows:

p4 Tony Lovell; **p11** Mark Steward; **p12** Jonny Young / Discovery Communications; **p14** Jon Williams (www.jon-w.com); **p18** Ed Stafford social media; **p20** Mark Steward; **p22** Greg Epperson / SS; **p24** Greg Epperson / SS; **p27** Mark A. Rice / SS; **p31** TravelNerd / SS; **p32** King Ropes Access / SS; **p34** oksana.perkins / SS (San Juan Islands, Washington State, USA); **p38** Michal Pancir / SS; **p40** PixieMe / SS; **p42** Mogens Trolle / SS; **p43** Andrey Armyagov / SS; **p45** Daniel Bruce Lacy / SS; **p46** Keith Ducatel; **p48** R.M. Nunes / SS; **p50** Keith Ducatel; **p54** evenfh / SS; **p56** Szczepan Klejbuk / SS; **p58** Jonas Tufvesson / SS; **p60** Jonas Tufvesson / SS; **p61** Catalin Grigoriu / SS; **p62** Jonas Tufvesson / SS; **p64** Jonas Tufvesson / SS; **p65** Gael Varoquaux / CC BY 2.0; **p66** VJ Villafranca / Discovery Communications (Palau); **p68** Lewis Pugh / image via Jason Roberts (North Pole); **p70** ALEKSANDR RIUTIN / SS; **p71** Katvic / SS; **p72** Katvic / SS; **p74** Andrey Nekrasov / Alamy Stock Photo; **p76** Anton Petrus / SS; **p79** Lewis Pugh / image via Kelvin Trautman; **p80** aaabbbccc / SS (En route, slowly, to Maroantsetra, Northern Madagascar); **p82** remzik / SS; **p84** aaabbbccc / SS; **p86** Travel Stock / SS; **p87** Jose HERNANDEZ Camera 51 / SS; **p88** Leonid Andronov / SS; **p91** aaabbbccc / SS; **p92** Masa Sakano / CC BY 2.0; **p96** Tom Pilgrim / SS; **p98** Paul A Carpenter / SS; **p100** Simon Dannhauer / SS; **p102** Strahil Dimitrov / SS; **p105** Christopher Jensen / CC BY 2.0; **p106** Fabian Plock / SS; **p107** Christopher Jensen / CC BY 2.0; **p108** Cloud Level Media / SS; **p110** Dmitry Naumov / SS; **p113** VJ Villafranca / Discovery Communications (Palau); **p114** Discovery Communications (Kimberley Coast, Western Australia); **p118** Izabela23 / SS; **p120** George W. Bailey / SS; **p121** Discovery Communications (Olorua, Fiji); **p122** loneroc / SS; **p124** Land Rover Our Planet; **p126** terekhov igor / SS; **p129** Marisa Estivill / SS; **p129** alessandro pinto / SS; **p130**; Peter van Evert / Alamy Stock; photo / Alamy Stock; photo; **p131** Laura Facchini / SS; **p132** KombiLife; **p133**

saiko3p / SS; **p134** Izzarshah Khan / SS; **p136** Aleynikov Pavel / SS; **p137** divedog / SS; **p138** Tami Freed / SS; **p141** Angelo Giampiccolo / SS; **p143** Ethan Daniels / SS; **p144** Jeff Stamer / SS; **p146** Sander van der Werf / SS; **p148** Courtesy Everett Collection / Alamy; **p150** Michael Hodge / CC BY 2.0; **p151** Michael Hodge / CC BY 2.0; **p152** Michael Hodge / CC BY 2.0; **p153** Jacob Resor / CC BY 2.0; **p154** tent86 / CC BY 2.0; **p157** VJ Villafranca / Discovery Communications (Palau); **p158** Somchai Siriwanarangson / SS (Elephant trekking in Northern Thailand); **p160** Ikpro / SS; **p164** VJ Villafranca / Discovery Communications (Ed in the Danakil); **p163** Ikpro / SS; **p166** Yongyut Kumsri / SS; **p168** THPStock / SS (Milford Track, New Zealand); **p172** Bob Wick / Bureau of Land Management / CC BY 2.0; **p175** Tobin Akehurst / SS; **p176** Mathilde R / SS; **p178** Roop Dey / SS (Varanasi, India); **p180** Lukasz Kurbiel / SS; **p182** Songquan Deng / SS; **p185** Kevin Poh / CC BY 2.0; **p187** Henk Bogaard / SS; **p188** jennyt / SS; **p189** Shardalow / CC BY 2.0; **p190** Fredi Bach / CC BY 2.0; **p194** Guillermo Olaizola / SS; **p196** Vadim Petrakov / SS; **p198** VJ Villafranca / Discovery Communications; **p200** phototravelua / SS (Yak Attack Race, Nepal); **p203** Cerveny Michal / Alamy Stock; photo; **p204** My Good Images / SS; **p205** Warren Rohner / CC BY 2.0; **p206** OHishiapply / SS; **p207** N/A / CC BY 2.0; **p208** phototravelua / SS; **p210** HuxleyMedia / SS; **p213** Voran / SS; **p216** Orlok / SS; **p218** Jake Sorensen / SS; **p220** Alberto Loyo / SS; **p221** Paula French / SS; **p222** Les Gibbon / Alamy Stock; photo; **p224** HPH Image Library / SS (Black Rhino, Kruger National; park); **p226** RPSP / SS (South Luangwa National; park); **p228** FCG / SS; **p229** kongsak sumano / SS; **p230** Muhammad Azham / SS (Hikers en route to K2 Base Camp); **p233** Joseph Sohm / SS; **p234** pakawat Thongcharoen / SS; **p236** Aggeich / SS; **p238**; Piotr Snigorski / SS; **p240** TripDeeDee Photo / SS; **p243** lebedev / SS; **p245** Mark Steward; **p246** Peiman Zekavat; **p248** Peiman Zekavat; **p249** Jon Williams (www.jon-w.com); **p250** Peiman Zekavat; **p251** Jon Williams (www.jon-w.com); **p252** Jon Williams (www.jon-w.com); **p253** De kwest / SS; **p254** Eva Vallespin / SS; **p256** orangecrush / SS; **p258** attilio pregnolato / SS; **p261** critterbiz / SS